Praise for *The Awakening of HK Derryberry*

"This is a story of one man's choice to love and invest in the life of a special-needs little boy and how that one choice transformed them both. You will laugh and cry and be moved to love even the unlikely, as Jim did, and never to give up, no matter what challenges you face, like HK. This heartwarming story will change you for good!"

—ALAN JACKSON,
GRAMMY AWARD–WINNING SINGER/SONGWRITER

"A true delight! Every person should read Jim Bradford and HK's touching story. Your heart will be uplifted, your soul awakened. It reminds us that every life carries enormous worth. I've had the pleasure of meeting HK— he inspires me! I'm certain his story will do the same for you."

—DAN T. CATHY
CHAIRMAN AND CEO, CHICK-FIL-A

"One of our biggest mistakes as humans is placing limits on people who are different than us; people who are like HK Derryberry. Born prematurely, HK is blind, has cerebral palsy, and has countless other challenges. Yet HK is the most incredible and unique person I have ever met in my life. If you ever meet him, I can promise you'll never forget him; and, because of his amazing memory, he won't forget you either. This book will inspire you to look deeper into the way you see others."

—SCOTT HAMILTON
OLYMPIC GOLD MEDALIST

"To think that this man, Jim Bradford, worked alongside us mere mortals was a revelation. How many other people out there are doing remarkable things with their lives right under our noses? Jim and HK's story is uplifting and an example of what love can do. It demonstrates how paying attention, and looking beyond human boundaries, can expose something greater than a physical body. It's the human spirit."

—CYNTHIA CROATTI
EXECUTIVE VICE PRESIDENT, UNIFIRST CORPORATION

"The journey of HK Derryberry and Jim Bradford is truly an amazing one, a moving story like no other you have ever heard. If this one doesn't warm your heart, check your pulse. The story of this unlikely duo—Bradford, a successful and stylish business executive, and a young blind boy with multiple disabilities and raised on the margins of society—will keep you turning pages well into the night. The results, seventeen years from their initial meeting, will surprise and inspire you to be more aware of the opportunities God puts in your path all the time."

—DR. ROYCE MONEY
CHANCELLOR, ABILENE CHRISTIAN UNIVERSITY

"Wow! This book is a must-read. And to think HK is my friend. What a joy it is to recommend this book to people of all ages. Jim and HK's story is making a difference in the lives of people everywhere."

—GENE STALLINGS
FORMER HEAD FOOTBALL COACH, UNIVERSITY OF ALABAMA

"As a scientist, I was completely blown away by HK's phenomenal ability to recall his past, but over time his story and our friendship transcended science. I am a better person for having known him and being able to call him my friend."

—DR. BRANDON ALLY
PROFESSOR OF NEUROLOGY, VANDERBILT UNIVERSITY

The Awakening of
HK DERRYBERRY

MY UNLIKELY FRIENDSHIP *with*
the BOY WHO REMEMBERS EVERYTHING

JIM BRADFORD

with ANDY HARDIN

W PUBLISHING GROUP

AN IMPRINT OF THOMAS NELSON

Published in Nashville, Tennessee, by W Publishing Group, an imprint of Thomas Nelson.

Thomas Nelson titles may be purchased in bulk for educational, business, fund-raising, or sales promotional use. For information, please e-mail SpecialMarkets@ThomasNelson.com.

The Scripture quotation marked NIV is taken from the Holy Bible, New International Version®, NIV®. © 1973, 1978, 1984, 2011 by Biblica, Inc.® Used by permission of Zondervan. All rights reserved worldwide.

The Scripture quotation marked NASB is taken from New American Standard Bible®. © 1960, 1962, 1963, 1968, 1971, 1972, 1973, 1975, 1977, 1995 by The Lockman Foundation. Used by permission.

Some material presented in chapter 32 is based on interviews with Dr. Brandon Ally in the fall of 2015 by Andy Hardin and a summer 2012 alumni magazine article that appeared in *Vanderbilt Medicine*, ed. Kathy Whitney, "The Amazing Life and Memory of H.K. Derryberry," written by Leslie Hill.

Library of Congress Cataloging-in-Publication Data

Names: Bradford, James L., 1943– author.
Title: The awakening of HK Derryberry : my unlikely friendship with the boy who remembers everything / Jim Bradford, with Andy Hardin.
Other titles: Awakening of H. K. Derryberry
Description: Nashville : W Publishing Group, 2016.
Identifiers: LCCN 2016008459 | ISBN 9780718079994 (hard cover : alk. paper)
Subjects: LCSH: Derryberry, HK. | Memory.
Classification: LCC BF371 .B734 2016 | DDC 973.932092/2 [B] —dc23
    LC record available at https://lccn.loc.gov/2016008459

Printed in the United States of America

16 17 18 19 20 RRD 6 5 4 3 2 1

Throw your heart over the fence and the rest will follow.
—NORMAN VINCENT PEALE

"I will lead the blind by ways they have not known,
along unfamiliar paths I will guide them;
I will turn the darkness into light before them
and make the rough places smooth.
These are the things I will do;
I will not forsake them."

—ISAIAH 42:16 NIV

Contents

—m—

CONTENTS

—◦◦—

An Aimless Existence

The small nine-year-old boy sat where he sat every weekend—in the fast-food dining room, at the same window table. He sat hunched, his ear close to the same old beat-up boom box that was held together with three strips of silver duct tape and tuned to one of two stations—sports-talk or Pentecostal preaching. A crooked antenna jutted out from the radio like the floppy ear of an old dog.

Pearl Derryberry, the boy's grandmother, coveted her part-time hours at Mrs. Winner's Chicken & Biscuits, especially since she had been reorganized out of her thirty-one-year career with the gas company. The modest severance and social security payments barely covered expenses for her and her grandson whom she was raising alone. Blind, with cerebral palsy, and paralyzed on his right side since birth, HK attended the Tennessee School for the Blind during the week. But without affordable weekend day care options,

Pearl had no choice but to bring him along to her fast-food restaurant job.

Pearl checked on him regularly during breaks in her nine-hour shifts, and at some time during the day, they usually ate together, as regular customers and strangers passed their table with hardly a glance. Invisible to the world, the small blind boy perched over his broken-down radio went unnoticed but to only a few. That's just the way life had been since the accident.

—⁂—

CHAPTER 1

A Twenty-Five-Cent
Cup of Coffee

My name is Jim Bradford. I grew up as the middle child of a rural northern Alabama family of five. Never in my wildest dreams could I have imagined my blessed life during the 1990s. My wife, Brenda, and I had been married thirty-five years and were proud parents of two beautiful, healthy daughters, Bridget and Julie. I enjoyed a productive and lucrative sales career in the textile industry, and once the girls were independent young women and out of the nest, Brenda and I looked forward to travel opportunities and checking off our bucket list of adventures we had postponed for years. Looking back now, I see that we had finally reached our definition of success, enjoying almost every material blessing we could want, and seriously pondering retirement.

———

We settled in Williamson County, Tennessee, in 1975, after a company transfer from Montgomery, Alabama. Williamson County is consistently ranked among the wealthiest in the nation and is also among the country's fastest-growing suburban areas. Large horse and cattle farms have given way to luxurious gated subdivisions, multi-storied office parks, and sprawling shopping malls, particularly in the northern area that borders metropolitan Nashville.

Our four-bedroom brick ranch house is situated in Brentwood, a comfortable bedroom community just eleven miles from downtown Music City. This shady one-acre corner lot was once part of a multi-generational family cattle farm with a history dating back to the Civil War. When we moved there, keeping my restored antique 1955 Chevrolet Bel Air in pristine operating condition ranked high on my weekly priority list. It was right up there with maintaining our immaculate lawn and landscape. The neighborhood homeowners' association conducted a weekly "Yard of the Week" contest from May through September. Their sign found its way onto our yard at least once every summer.

We stayed plenty busy, but I made time for weekly tennis matches with a group of longtime friends. The neighborhood swim and tennis club just two blocks down the street continued to be a summer magnet for our family. Subdivision traffic was practically non-existent most days, leaving ample opportunity for walkers, joggers, bikers, and baby-strolling mothers. All dogs were leashed. Barney Fife, with his single bullet, would have been right at home in our idyllic, crime-free neighborhood.

We enjoyed a simple lifestyle, certainly not luxurious by any-one's imagination. We drove older, well-maintained vehicles. Our lives revolved around church, and you could find us, like many good Southerners, at church at least three times a week, and more on special occasions. Actually, I had always considered myself ordinary in every conceivable way, no better or worse than our friends and neighbors. But no doubt, God had richly blessed our family.

It was an unseasonably cool fifty-five degrees on Saturday, October 16, 1999, in my little corner of paradise. I suppose that was one reason I suddenly craved a cup of hot coffee that morning. I usually limited my daily caffeine intake to just one cup, and I had already reached my quota, thanks to the Golden Arches. But today was different. I needed more.

Winding up our usual tennis match by midmorning, my thoughts wandered to an extended list of Saturday chores awaiting me, so I quickly said good-bye to my tennis partners. Without thinking, I took the longest, most time-consuming and out-of-the-way route to Brentwood. I drove slowly, observing the charming old estates along Tyne Boulevard. My leisurely driving pace, combined with Garrison Keillor's distinctive radio voice, mysteriously intensified my coffee desire as I turned south onto Hillsboro Road. Visions of Starbucks flashed before my eyes.

I drove five miles, following my usual route east on Old Hickory Boulevard. At the Franklin Road intersection, my next decision was easy: turn right, drive one mile to Starbucks, and pay $2.00 for a cup of coffee. Curiously, abruptly, and without thinking, I turned left and drove a short distance across a narrow bridge over a railroad gulch to a small fast-food restaurant near the edge of the Brentwood city limits. Mrs. Winner's Chicken & Biscuits was a fried-chicken joint that just happened to serve breakfast. I had eaten there once or twice, but for the life of me, I don't ever remember stopping there just for coffee.

The undersized parking lot accommodated only a few cars, but fortunately I landed a spot directly across from the building's entrance. I quickly cut the ignition and darted for warmth inside as a steady north wind made the overcast day feel even colder.

———

Surprisingly, I was the only counter customer that Saturday morning. Walking toward the cashier, I caught a glimpse of a small boy sitting alone by the dining room window. I looked away as I focused on my order. I spotted the restaurant's menu hanging from a colorful placard behind the counter. Another sign above the iced tea dispenser announced, "Maxwell House Coffee Served Here. Good to the Last Drop!"

"I'd like a cup of coffee, please," I said.

"Are you fifty-five years old?" came the reply.

That's a mighty strange question to ask someone, I thought to myself. *It's not like I'm buying alcohol and need to be carded.* Then I heard echoes of Brenda's frequent complaints about my need for hearing aids and wondered if I heard her correctly. Slightly bewildered, I turned around, thinking she might have been speaking to someone behind me. Realizing that I was indeed the lone customer in an otherwise empty fast-food restaurant, I answered feebly, "Yes."

The cashier, a short, stocky lady about my age with close-cropped gray hair, informed me that at age fifty-five, based on restaurant rules, I qualified as a senior citizen. She announced that my newly bestowed citizenship in that not-very-exclusive club entitled me to a cup of coffee for twenty-five cents, a whopping twenty-seven cents with tax! I briefly considered renouncing my citizenship just to maintain my youthful self-image but soon realized it was time to stop living an illusion. I thanked her and paid for my first cup of senior coffee.

The aroma of fresh-brewed java and hot buttermilk biscuits filled the restaurant. As I turned to leave, I was drawn back to the small silhouette I had barely noticed just two minutes earlier. From this angle I could clearly see that it was a young boy. He was not eating. Turning a corner, I saw his head pressed down over a black plastic boom box with silver dials and a broken antenna. Three strips of duct tape held the battery cover in place. My prying eyes were drawn to the long, white plastic braces on each leg. Even from a distance I knew this boy had problems.

—∞—

CHAPTER 2

The Pint-Sized Pickpocket

I can't explain why, but the sight of that little boy stirred emotions deep within my soul. Though I had never known anyone with special needs, I had always noticed special-needs children in public places. But I was never quite brave enough to acknowledge them or their caregivers. My first reaction had always been sympathy, followed closely by relief, and finally, thankfulness for my healthy family. Today my spirit took me in a different direction, one that seemed out of character for me. Instead of simply walking away as I had done so many times before, I felt a gentle nudge moving me toward this little boy.

As I tossed my stir-stick into the nearest trash can, I turned and noticed another restaurant employee. A slender young woman with fiery red hair stood behind the counter loading plastic utensils into a large cardboard container. According to the name badge pinned to her red T-shirt festooned with a large yellow chicken, she was Helen.

"Helen, who's the little boy sitting at that table?" I asked hesitantly.

She smiled and replied, "Oh, that's HK; he's our sweetheart. He's Pearl's grandson."

"Who's Pearl?" I inquired.

"She's our cashier," Helen said, pointing to the smiling woman standing at the opposite end of the counter, the same woman who had just presented me with my first senior coffee. It was absolutely none of my business, but the sight of this young boy sitting alone in an empty dining area, listening to his radio puzzled me, and I had to learn more.

"What's her grandson doing here?" I quietly questioned.

"HK lives with Pearl. She doesn't have a weekend babysitter, so he comes to work with her," Helen patiently replied.

"How long does he sit here?"

"Oh, usually just from eight to five."

Instantly and without thinking, I exclaimed, "You've got to be kidding me! He sits there for nine hours each day?"

Helen's look and response came with a defiant tone. "He goes to school during the week while Pearl works; he doesn't just sit there every day!"

Her next statement caught me totally off guard and shook me hard. "He's blind and has cerebral palsy."

My chin began to quiver, and a large tear formed in my right eye. Suddenly the fresh cup of coffee no longer seemed important. Gently, slowly, I moved toward his table to get a better view. He appeared smaller than when I first noticed him, and based on his size I thought he looked no more than five or six years old. His buzz haircut was long overdue for a trim, and he wore a plain cotton T-shirt stained on the front with what looked like remnants of breakfast. But I was most shocked by the wrinkled khaki cargo shorts he wore on this unseasonably cold October morning.

Moving even closer, I got a better look at the white plastic braces supporting the lower parts of both legs. These were unlike any braces I'd ever seen. They were firmly inserted into his shoes and extended up his calves to just below the knee. Long white cotton tube socks were pulled up his legs to within an inch of the top of the braces.

"Hey, buddy," I said softly as I reached his table.

"What's your name?" he replied.

"My name is Jim. What's your name?"

"I'm HK."

"What does HK stand for?"

"Nothing, just HK."

"HK, it's nice to meet you."

"It's nice to meet you too. Where do you live?"

"In Brentwood."

"What street do you live on?"

"Harpeth River Drive."

"What's that off of?"

"Old Hickory Boulevard," I answered.

"What time did you get up this morning?" HK inquired.

"Six o'clock," I replied.

"What did you do when you got up?"

"I took a shower."

"What did you do next?"

"I got dressed."

"What did you do next?"

"I drove to McDonald's to meet my tennis partners."

He continued this tough line of questioning like a relentless seasoned detective. After a few minutes of his incessant interrogation, I thought to myself, *Wow, this is one funny little kid!*

He kept pounding me with questions, and I kept responding. During one short pause, he took my hand and gently rubbed it with his fingers as though exploring a delicate art object. Then he brought it to his nose, like a puppy playfully sniffing its owner, committing my unique identifying scent to memory. After about fifteen minutes, I had to leave.

"I enjoyed meeting you, HK. I have errands to run and need to go."

"I hope I can see you again sometime," he said hesitantly.

"Me too," I replied with a sizable lump in my throat.

Turning to leave my newfound friend, I became an innocent victim to the biggest thief in town. Like a pickpocket honing his stealthy craft among the gawking tourists of Nashville's downtown honky-tonks, HK Derryberry had committed the perfect crime: he stole my heart.

My mind raced through the long list of Saturday chores ahead, mostly honey-dos for Brenda. I walked much slower than when I first arrived. The weather, the traffic, the time of day all seemed like a blur to me. I left Mrs. Winner's parking lot, but I could not ditch thoughts of this little blind boy. Just thinking about him broke my heart and brought me to tears. I realized my compelling cup of hot coffee remained untouched, but I did not care.

Questions flooded my head the remainder of that day. I chuckled as I replayed his intense interrogation. I even had a few questions of my own: *Where were his parents? How bad were his health problems? Where did he live?* I found myself driving aimlessly while attempting to complete my weekend errand list. Images of his forlorn face, dirty clothes, and white leg braces became seared into my brain. Since I was without tissues, my warm-up jacket sleeve doubled as a handkerchief for my tear-filled eyes. I knew absolutely nothing about him or his life, except his weekend day care at Mrs. Winner's.

Eventually I completed my errands and ended up back home. Placing the grocery bags on our kitchen counter, I shared news of the unexpected encounter with my wife. I gushed about the funny little boy, his sad appearance, and his endless questions. She had no response, so I never mentioned him again that weekend. Sunday's church sermon about meaningful life relationships struck another of my emotional chords, and again I struggled to fight back tears.

—ᴍ—

Groundhog Day

Tennis season at Belle Meade Country Club's indoor center ran from October through February. Eight close buddies and I rotated doubles partners most Saturday mornings for an eight thirty, best two-out-of-three match. Each player was scheduled one Saturday off a month, and my next free Saturday greeted me with gray skies and a steady north wind, making it feel colder than my carport thermometer reading. After a late-morning breakfast, I bundled in layers, found my work gloves and a warm stocking cap, and proceeded outside to reclaim my territory from a yard full of orphaned leaves that had invaded my spotless corner lot.

As I was raking, my thoughts drifted back to HK, something they had done every day since we had met. I wondered about his home life, whether he was sitting alone at Mrs. Winner's, and how many innocent victims he had interrogated that morning. I remembered my daughters at his age and how my expecting them to sit calmly in a room for more than five minutes without television or other distractions would have been inconceivable. They had no more ability to endure that kind of solitude than I had surviving twelve rounds with a heavyweight boxer. Yet that intrepid, or incredibly patient, young boy sat alone in that dreary restaurant for nine excruciating hours every Saturday and Sunday because his grandmother had no other weekend options. My brain simply could not fathom his misery.

By midafternoon I had stuffed forty large contractor's bags full of leaves and neatly stacked the bags streetside. Errant backyard strays taunted me, but I was cold, tired, and done. I put away my rake, changed jackets, replaced the stocking cap with my favorite blue Auburn ball cap, and told Brenda that I was going out for coffee. I don't recall mentioning Mrs. Winner's.

The trip to the restaurant took only ten minutes. As I entered the parking lot, I spied HK sitting alone at the window, exactly where I had left him last week. Just seeing his small head once again stirred my emotions. I felt relief that he was there and was strangely giddy at the thought of seeing him again. What did I expect from this visit? What had I come to do? I really didn't know for sure; I just knew that the urge to come back and see this boy was overwhelming. But this time I determined I would be the one asking all the questions.

I rushed into the restaurant to escape another blast of cold air, claimed my senior coffee, and ambled into the dining room. As I approached HK, it appeared that he wore the same clothes as last week—a droopy white cotton T-shirt with faded cargo shorts that were a size too small. Rounding out his wardrobe were those white plastic leg braces and odd black shoes that looked as though they came straight out of my grandmother's closet.

Tiptoeing closer, I detected a moist, three-inch stain in the middle of his soiled T-shirt, no doubt residue from his lunch. He was completely mesmerized by sounds pounding from his dilapidated music box. His upper body strained over the table, his head cocked to one side, struggling to listen with one ear while eavesdropping on nearby table conversations with the other. The volume was low enough that customers weren't disturbed, but drawing closer, I recognized the pulsating, singsong voice of a Pentecostal preacher. These distinctive sound waves, springing deep from within the bowels of some middle Tennessee basement studio, held the impressionable young boy utterly transfixed. He swayed in perfect rhythm with the rise and fall of the evangelist's voice, hanging on every "Praise God!" and "Hallelujah!" that came through the speaker.

In a week his hair had grown enough to make his tiny face look even smaller than I remembered. He could have passed easily for a five-year-old, although at our last visit he had revealed to me that his ninth birthday was in July. He heard me approaching, but before I could speak, my chin began to quiver as I valiantly fought torrents of emotion. He raised his head and appeared to look me in the eye.

"What's your name?" he asked in a high-pitched squeaky voice.

"I'm Jim," I replied.

"Are you the same man I talked to last Saturday?"

"Yes I am; you sure have a good memory."

"Where do you live?"

"In Brentwood."

"What street do you live on?"

"Harpeth River Drive."

"What's that off of?"

"Old Hickory Boulevard." (Eventually I discovered that if he was unfamiliar with a street name, he inquired about adjoining streets until he recognized one. Only then would he proceed to the next set of questions.)

"What time did you get up this morning?"

———

"Six o'clock."

"What did you do when you got up?"

"I showered."

"What did you do next?"

"I got dressed."

"What did you do next?"

"I worked in my yard raking leaves."

"What did you do next?"

Any notion that I would assume the interrogator role this time around instantly vanished. He repeated the same basic questions each time we met. I felt like Phil Connors in the movie *Groundhog Day*, tortuously looping the same twenty-four hours over and over again. Like Phil, I soon anticipated the repetitive drill and became determined to change it. So after my second or third visit, I began responding with something like, "I answered that question last week, and my routine doesn't change very much. So let's talk about something else." I tried drawing him into normal two-way dialogue, but I failed miserably each time.

Finally it dawned on me: HK's lack of social contact with anyone except Pearl had severely restricted his development of normal communication skills. Simply put, he was a social virgin, unable to converse on any topic except those that Pearl had discussed in his presence or that he had heard from radio or television. It seemed that God was presenting me with a blank canvas, leaving it to me to complete the picture.

Later during that second visit, he gently grasped my hand as he had before and, while holding it close to his face, explored each finger as if committing my scent to memory. His enhanced olfactory ability allowed him to identify me and other acquaintances from quite a distance. Nervously I fully expected a similar exploration of my face, but it never happened.

———

Within a short time he was able to instantly recognize me when I would walk into the restaurant dining room, greeting me with "Hi, Mr. Bradford!" before I could utter a word. I noticed in particular that since our first meeting, he always referred to me as "Mr. Bradford." He addressed everyone else by his or her first name, but not me, and I don't have a clue as to why.

During subsequent visits, I realized I was not the only Mrs. Winner's customer affected by the little blind boy's presence at the window table. I occasionally discovered money, usually a ten- or twenty-dollar bill, carefully folded and tucked underneath his battered boom box. Upon my inquiry he would say, "I don't know anything about it. I didn't know there was money on my table. How much is it?"

Decent human beings had obviously noticed the little boy hiding in plain sight and wanted to help in some small way. I wondered how many others saw him, walked away, and did nothing. I'll be the first to admit that my righteous scorecard in that game was next to zero until meeting HK. I could not tally the innumerable times I had looked beyond a downtown homeless man asking for meal money or drove blankly past a disheveled veteran holding a "Will Work for Food" sign in the middle of a busy Nashville intersection. Believe me, I know what it's like to discount the poor and close my eyes to the marginalized hiding among us. But God had given me a second chance, and I had something to offer this go-round: compassion, care, and lots of time.

HK's desolate weekends at the restaurant and a monotonous home life disturbed me and upset the comfort I had enjoyed in our peaceful corner of the world. I felt a gentle hand pushing, stirring, and prodding. God had me exactly where He wanted me.

CHAPTER 4

—⚶—

"I'll Never Forget You for the Rest of My Life"

My friendship with the young blind boy with disabilities blossomed quickly in spite of our forty-seven-year age difference. Regular sessions at the now-familiar window table made us look and sound like two crusty old farmers holding court in the middle of the restaurant.

Once, HK gently found my right hand with his left and, without warning, quietly uttered, "Mr. Bradford, I love you. You are my best friend. When you die, I will never forget you for the rest of my life."

I wish I knew what prompted this surprise declaration, but it caught me completely off guard. I was reduced to a river of tears, and after clearing my throat, I responded, "Thank you, HK. I love you too. I hope I live a long time so we can continue to be good friends for many more years."

He turned, faced me, and broke into the biggest, brightest, most heartwarming smile I had ever witnessed. Perhaps he sensed that for the first time in his life he had found a genuine friend other than his grandmother. From that time on HK spontaneously referred to me as his best friend, sometimes completing this thought with "I love you, Mr. Bradford."

Soon both days of the weekend found me following the familiar route and returning to the Mrs. Winner's parking lot. If his face was not visible in the window, I would forgo my coffee purchase, drive around the building, and return home. I understood why HK was sometimes not there—Pearl was not scheduled to work every weekend. These rare occasions left me empty in more ways than one.

But on the days I spotted his usual silhouette, I was euphoric. I always anticipated our time together. Over a cup of senior coffee for me and sweet iced tea for him, we would discuss my job, my travels, and my family while I squeezed out tidbits of personal information about his school, his friends and family, his likes and dislikes. I learned, for example, that his favorite Mrs. Winner's meal was sausage and gravy dished over a well-done buttered biscuit. It was normally served only during breakfast hours, but thanks to his "inside" connections, he could order his favorite meal anytime. As a result of these developing two-way conversations, I began to notice encouraging signs of his emerging personality. The more we interacted, the more his conversational skills improved.

Weekend visits strengthened my friendship with HK and gave me opportunities to observe the full range of his emotional spectrum. One Saturday afternoon I witnessed a scene that I suspect many working parents have experienced. Saying good-bye and walking out the door on an extended business trip can be brutal, especially for young children. Sometimes these partings result in meltdowns of epic proportions.

Each time I left Mrs. Winner's, I gave HK a huge bear hug and told him how much I enjoyed our visit. He always returned the favor, but on this particular afternoon he wrapped his small arms around me and tearfully begged for me not to leave. His sudden, frantic response was simply unbearable and brought tears to my eyes. He became inconsolable to the point of disturbing nearby customers and caused such a heartbreaking scene that Pearl had to abandon her cash register and come to my rescue. She calmly reassured him that I was not leaving forever. "Mr. Bradford needs to go now, but he will come back to see you again soon."

Pearl's shift was almost over, so I stayed with him until she got off work. I grabbed his left hand on our way out the front door and gently helped him walk to Pearl's pickup truck parked behind the restaurant. I opened the door, lifted his fifty-three-pound frame into the passenger seat, and securely fastened his seat belt. At that point his distress ceased. It seemed the clicking sound gave him reassurance that not only was his safety firmly intact, but our friendship was as well.

The next week Pearl made it a point to tell me the story behind his meltdown. "Until HK met you, every other person he has encountered at the restaurant—or anyone else for that matter—who has shown him the least bit of affection suddenly disappears and has never returned. That includes both his father and grandfather. Now he considers you his best friend, and I think he's afraid you'll do the same thing one day."

Knowing this sad fact enabled me to understand the traumatic incident, but it did not erase the memory of my fragile emotions when he refused to let me go. Even today the word *good-bye* is noticeably absent from his vocabulary. Instead, his standard reply to anyone leaving him is "Take care."

Without question I was now in way over my head, in deep water. To validate my buddy's abandonment issues by turning away from him was no longer an option. At this point I could no more withdraw from him than I could renounce my American citizenship. But my dilemma was that I already had an adoring, caring family whom I loved. I prayed for divine guidance and fervently searched for answers.

No doubt the casual observer would find this sprouting friendship a bit unusual. In fact, that was the expressed opinion of one person in particular who was much more than a casual observer. As HK and I grew increasingly close, my wife questioned my sanity and raised more than a few objections. She observed a fifty-six-year-old man and father of two grown daughters eagerly anticipating another encounter with a nine-year-old boy who had several disabilities and who was neither his son nor a family relative. Brenda knew that I thought about him frequently during most waking hours. HK stories spilled out to our circle of friends; no story was too insignificant to share with them. I just could not say enough about him to anyone who would listen. She took full notice of my growing obsession, letting me know that I was quickly becoming overly attached to the cute little youngster.

My constant preoccupation with HK was affecting our marriage and our social life. It left little room for anyone or anything else, including Brenda and our friends. Her outgoing personality yearned for weekends as a couple, card games with friends, boating and social outings. Hearing—but most important, *listening to*—her concerns, I knew I was guilty as charged. Something had to change. Brenda and I needed time together, including social activity with friends, so we decided to make Friday evenings our special night as a couple.

CHAPTER 5

—∽—

Precious Pearl and the Family Tree

Pearl Derryberry—Grammy, as HK called her—occasionally joined my tableside conversations with HK during her breaks. Slowly I began to absorb important bits of family information about HK and his grandmother. They could count on one hand the number of friends and acquaintances they had between the two of them. Their bankrupt social life consisted of incidental talk with the restaurant regulars.

I'm confident Pearl enjoyed our sporadic moments of fellowship as much as HK did. She had a lifetime of heartbreaking stories to share but no one to share them with. She was an excellent storyteller, and I was an attentive listener. Often her stories would drift back in time to her own early years or take a dark turn when she mentioned "the accident"—an event that had obviously changed everything. Growing more comfortable with me, she did most of the talking while I listened and scooped up crumbs of information. She shared painful stories about her parents, a disastrous marriage, and her two sons. I heard about childhood memories on the farm, her previous job, and a heap of stories about HK. Naturally, I wondered what had happened to HK's parents, and it was midafternoon one Saturday after the lunch crowd had thinned and Pearl was on a long lunch break that the time came for her to drop the bombshell I'd been waiting to hear. The dining room was quiet, and she had a captive audience.

I listened as she shared the heartbreaking tale. She recollected pieces of the story from her own experience, while other snippets had been scooped up and fit together like a puzzle from tidbits that her son William had shared over time. Even now she admitted not knowing every detail of the events she did not personally experience, but that did not stop her from weaving the story in great detail.

Growing up as an only child and a "plain ole country girl," Pearl knew the meaning of work, especially when her daddy needed farm help. She couldn't wait to escape her mundane country life in Maury County, Tennessee, and move on to a brighter future in the big city of Nashville. Plenty smart in school, Pearl developed into a short, stocky young woman in perfect proportions for farmwork but not so much for attracting the opposite sex.

She shared a rambunctious gene that ran from root to stem in her family tree. Over her parents' vehement objection, she eloped with the first man she ever dated and at age nineteen promptly started married life in Illinois. Even then she admitted her gullibility and the fact that she was easy pickings for any man to sweep her off her feet. Reflecting on her poor life choices, she offered a unique philosophical viewpoint: "I took out a loan in life at age nineteen that I'm still paying interest on." You could call it "Pearl's Pearl of Wisdom."

Their marriage lasted two years and three days from start to finish, of which she and John might have spent six months together. He was an over-the-road trucker filled with wanderlust and a fiery temper. Despite scant time together as husband and wife, their union produced two boys born thirteen months apart. William, their firstborn, was a carbon copy of his no-account, irresponsible father. She was thankful that Jimmy, her baby, inherited more of his mama's genes.

When the doomed marriage finally disintegrated, Pearl and her boys returned to Tennessee. She was dead set on erasing any remnants of her failed life with John, so she took the extraordinary step of petitioning a Tennessee court to permanently restore the Derryberry name to both her offspring. She landed an entry-level accounting job with the then Nashville Gas Company and settled alone in the city while her boys lived on their grandparents' Maury County farm more than an hour away. Thanks to the ex-husband, who stole her car during a feeble reconciliation attempt with his sons, she had no choice but to hitch a Greyhound bus every weekend to see her boys. Twenty-five years would pass before they would see John again.

Jimmy adjusted to farm life under his grandparents' roof and trudged through school seemingly unscathed by any remnant of his family history. But William's reputation as a hellion, just as his daddy had been, remained securely intact.

William's rebellious teenage years found him hanging with wisecracking outsiders and ending up on the wrong side of the law. He acquired a craving for drugs and a thirst for alcohol early in life. Drinking gave him such pretentious swagger and superior arrogance that even he probably believed the outrageous tales he spun to his buddies. He had no interest in school, eventually dropping out before finishing tenth grade.

———

Ten years later, after a nineteen-month stint in the army, a failed marriage, and prison time, William Howard Derryberry ran across Mary Kay Moon Davidson and liked what he saw. Her background was no better than his. Mary's hardworking parents labored long hours trucking cargo cross-country, away from home days at a time, leaving little time for parenting a precocious young girl like her. She had never experienced a nurturing, loving family or anything close to strong familial bonds.

Mary had always survived by masquerading as a woman in a child's body. She developed physically much younger than other girls her age and had attracted men's attention since grade school. Like most girls, Mary desperately yearned for her parents' affection, attention, and affirmation, especially her father's. Her dark hair, olive skin, and radiant smile made it easy to turn a man's head—and she was good at it. Mary had few girlfriends and nothing in common with any of them, so she ended up a teenage outcast. Predictably, she dropped out of school before completing seventh grade without any objection from her absentee parents. She became pregnant at age fourteen and promptly gave up her first child for adoption.

Though separated by just a few country miles, Mary never set eyes on William until after her eighteenth birthday. Their brief courtship became just another stop along the twisted road to adulthood. They began living together, unmarried, where their affair ensnared them in the same dysfunctional life cycle that had its roots deep within each of their family trees. They set up house in a small, weather-beaten rental near the end of a narrow two-lane country road in a remote corner of rural Maury County.

Maury County, sprinkled with country towns named Fly, Santa Fe (pronounced "Santa Fee"), Culleoka, Sawdust, and Hampshire, has been home to generations of hardscrabble tobacco and cattle farmers who have worked the same rich dirt that witnessed death

---

28

and destruction as Civil War battlefields just 125 years ago. Barely thirty minutes south of Nashville, Maury County has given the art of country music plenty of life to imitate. A visit to any of its backwater towns is enough to make one realize that every cliché lyric writ large in any real country song isn't just some fiction set to music. It is reality, straight from hundreds of communities just like these.

Like her companion, Mary acquired a taste for alcohol early in life. Maybe it provided hope and eased her pain; maybe she self-medicated to escape her present reality and terrible childhood memories; maybe alcohol temporarily pacified her lust for happiness. Whatever the reason, at age nineteen, Mary found herself hopelessly spiraling out of control yet again. Just two months after meeting the twenty-six-year-old farmhand, the now-familiar Walmart pregnancy test disclosed what she already knew—another baby was on the way. With no long-term commitment from William, Mary's future looked more hopeless than ever.

CHAPTER 6

—∞—

Quittin' Time

The thermometer was doing its best to shove the mercury above 100 degrees on the afternoon of Saturday, July 7, 1990. In middle Tennessee, July is a month of scorching, humid days and hot, steamy nights; a month when lush green lawns die without water and don't recover until the next spring; a month when churchgoing farmers pray more fervently than usual over their wilting crops; a month when city dogs stay cool indoors and country dogs stay cool under the house.

William and his farm crew had baled hay since early morning. It was almost quitting time. For William and the younger hands who never fretted a minute over finances, the day's pay would be their admission to a raucous evening of drinks and shooting eight-ball at the local beer joint. Two twenties and a ten elevated these workers to the top of the income bracket compared to other watering-hole regulars. On most Saturday nights the bar tab emptied wallets long before the next payday—or sometimes before the evening ended. Nevertheless, for William and his buddies, this was an acceptable way of life: week to week, payday to payday. You could call it his daddy's legacy.

The pregnancy had made Mary tired, so she had spent most of that Saturday morning in bed. But eventually she got up and dragged herself into the shower. She would dutifully have the car there by the field, waiting for William at quitting time, but what she desperately wanted was a night out on the town with her man. She walked through the kitchen, where at least a dozen Mountain Dew and Budweiser cans littered the counter as they did much of the rest of the cluttered rental house. On her way out the door, she picked up their Coleman cooler. She opened the car trunk and tossed aside an assorted collection of empty and smashed cans just to make room for the cooler. Mary smiled, knowing a quick detour for beer and ice would be the greatest gift she could give William that day.

The beat-up Hyundai had seen better days, but at least it was transportation. Just four weeks earlier Mary had totaled William's newer model in a two-car wreck that left her with bruises, minor scratches, and a mild concussion. Fortunately, her unborn child escaped unharmed. She faintly remembered hearing the emergency room doctor comment that her failure to wear a seat belt had probably saved the baby's life. She had not buckled up since that accident.

Heading down the dusty gravel drive, Mary turned left onto the main paved road. The speedometer eventually reached sixty-five as she drove into the sun on Carter's Creek Pike. The air conditioner didn't work, so all four windows were down. The front tires were practically bald and slightly out of balance, causing a gentle shimmy in the steering wheel. But at this point Mary didn't care. Her main objective was getting to a good time and a night out on the town.

Normally the trip took thirty minutes, but today she made it in twenty. Parking beneath two large sycamores, she opened the driver's door and waited. A slight breeze rustled through the trees as she cranked up Merle Haggard on the radio and planned their exciting night ahead. William arrived dog-tired, his Wrangler jeans and long-sleeved work shirt dirty and sweat stained from lifting sixty-five-pound hay bales since early morning. He had toiled hard for ten solid hours, loading wagon after wagon with the rectangular bales, stacking them in a stifling-hot, dusty barn loft, so just seeing Mary and her growing baby bump made his day. The ice-cold cargo waiting in the car trunk had its desired effect. He was one happy camper.

His lunch that day had consisted of a single slice of bologna on two pieces of white bread, two Hostess Twinkies, and a Mountain Dew. Five hours later he was exhausted, dehydrated, and hungry. As he had proven time and again, beer was an acceptable food substitute, one that satisfied his hunger a single cold can at a time.

Soon there were few unopened beers remaining in the cooler, but neither William nor Mary cared. Each swish and foam eased William's aches and made the sweltering workday seem like a faint memory. Mary had little trouble persuading him to enjoy a big night out with dinner and drinks, but first he needed to clean up and change clothes. Settling in for the drive home, she snuggled close to him as he drove, resting her hand on his right thigh. Her seat belt lay untouched.

The posted speed limit on this stretch of county road was fifty miles per hour, but with no traffic or law in sight, William inched the accelerator steadily downward until the speedometer topped out at seventy-five. His preoccupation with Mary's hand, idle thoughts of their evening ahead, and reflexes dulled by alcohol left him unprepared for the upcoming curvy stretch of Carter's Creek Pike.

—︾—

CHAPTER 7

Life-Giving Decision

Right on cue, Sir Isaac Newton's first law of motion kicked in and the speeding car failed to maneuver the second curve. Skidding out of control, the Hyundai violently spun as the rear of the car slammed full force into an ancient white oak tree. Instantly, the faded trunk and rusty fenders folded together like the flattened cans Mary had pitched from the trunk earlier that day. Glass shattered into thousands of small pieces the size of diamonds. Doors buckled and flew open, ejecting Mary's unharnessed body like a hurtled stone. The mighty oak stood oblivious as somewhere inside the mangled metal mess, hissing sounds faded into silence.

The nearest help would come from an approaching motorist who, at that moment, was out of sight and over a mile away. When the shocked rescuer arrived at the horrendous scene, he found Mary's motionless body lying on the ground, her head resting in a spreading pool of blood. William remained securely harnessed behind the wheel, dazed but not seriously hurt. Blood trickled down his chin, his lip cut from the steering wheel.

Mary clung to life while the unheralded motorist frantically dialed 911 on his portable Motorola phone. Within fifteen minutes a Maury County EMS unit from nearby Columbia arrived and immediately observed that Mary had suffered severe head trauma and desperately needed critical medical treatment. William was transported to Maury Regional Hospital, where he was treated and released with only minor injuries. Mary was airlifted to Vanderbilt University Medical Center, where a world-class medical facility and highly trained specialists awaited her arrival. The skilled helicopter trauma crew stabilized her for the twenty-three-minute flight to the hospital's medical tower landing pad.

Family members were contacted, and both mothers, along with William, rushed to Vanderbilt's medical complex in midtown Nashville. Doctors gave Mary's family scant hope that she would survive the night. A compassionate medical specialist counseled the distraught family, preparing them for the worst. Brain activity was nonexistent, and without the vast array of medical equipment surrounding her, pushing and pulling life into her lifeless body, she would already have died. Because Mary's insurmountable head injuries left virtually no hope for her survival, the doctor gently led the family to concentrate their attention on her unborn, yet still viable, fetus.

Speaking in simple terms, the doctor explained that even without trauma, a baby born three months early entered the world with odds unfairly stacked against him or her. Syndromes associated with Mary's alcohol use, coupled with a lack of prenatal care, created even greater odds against a healthy baby. A second doctor joined the conversation, and together they chronicled many potential ailments this baby would likely encounter. The lengthy list included underdeveloped lungs and heart, stroke, blindness, and brain damage, each problem likely requiring a lifetime of special care, assuming survival. They also mentioned that the baby's odds of living longer than a few days were extremely low. Given all these options, Mary's dazed mother looked hopelessly into the doctors' eyes and instructed them to do what they could to save the baby.

The specialized neonatal intensive care team kicked into high gear and feverishly prepared the delivery room for an emergency birth. At 6:01 on Sunday morning, July 8, 1990, a baby boy was born via cesarean section to William Derryberry and Mary Davidson. Two hours and twenty-nine minutes later, the life-sustaining apparatus connecting Mary's bruised and swollen body to her remaining semblance of life was disconnected. Her head trauma and other internal injuries proved too severe for any hope of recovery. William caressed her soft, swollen hand for the last time and sobbed uncontrollably as Mary drew her final breath.

Her unnamed son clung to his own frail life just down the hall from his mother. Outside the hospital on this sultry July Sunday morning, bell tower chimes from Belmont United Methodist Church filled the air with solemn yet joyous sounds, mourning death and celebrating birth.

The baby boy, delivered thirteen weeks early and weighing in at barely two pounds, arrived fighting from his first breath. He could have been appropriately named Rocky because of his stubborn struggle for life, but after three days he was given his father's first name, William. His middle name was a combination of the first initial of both parents' middle names. Though legally recorded as "William HK Derryberry" in the county clerk's office, he would simply be known as HK.

CHAPTER 8

—∞—

Miracle Baby

As Pearl spoke, I found myself sitting on the edge of my chair, both spellbound and appalled at learning of the unfolding tragedy surrounding HK's ill-fated entrance into the world. But that was just the beginning. There would be more to his story than heredity and birth.

Our Saturday sessions lasted several weekends as Pearl unloaded her storehouse of memories, and I learned how this miraculous little blind boy came to be sitting at that dining room table the day I entered the restaurant.

From the outset, the premature infant's survival was a daily struggle, touch-and-go at best. Pearl knew that William would never be fit for fatherhood, especially for a child who would require constant care and attention. His life consisted of a continual bounce between short-term menial employment and the county jail. So Pearl, at age forty-five, defaulted as her grandson's guardian.

———

Raising a special-needs grandchild as a single mother, while struggling to make ends meet, was hardly the life Pearl Derryberry envisioned. But she accepted the task, doggedly determined to be a better parent for her tiny, fragile grandson than she had been for her own two boys. She felt the accident had handed her a do-over, and she intended to take full advantage of it.

Wisely, Pearl had purchased a small two-bedroom, white frame house just east of downtown Nashville in 1986, after an unexpected promotion at the gas company. Her house was exactly seven miles from Vanderbilt Medical Center's neonatal intensive care unit, where HK spent the first three months of his life. Hospital protocol required on-duty personnel to log the name, date, and time of arrival and departure of every visitor entering the NICU. Pearl Derryberry's name is recorded there each of the ninety-six days her grandson struggled for life.

Some days she stopped by the hospital on her way to or from work. On days that HK's condition worsened and she had no time off, she used an extended lunch break to check on him. When those restless, lonely nights came and she found herself staring at the walls instead of sleeping, a short trip to the hospital provided solace and quieted the ever-present anxiety hovering just beyond her reach.

Pearl knew only a handful of people in Nashville, all gas company coworkers. Her aging mother, fighting her own health battles, occasionally ventured up from the farm to help keep the hospital vigil. William sporadically faded in and out of the picture but mostly out. Since the accident, he had tangled with his own unfathomable demons. Truth be told, Pearl climbed that insurmountable mountain alone. Isolated, without a support system, devoid of family and friends, she managed one hour, one day, one step at a time.

As Pearl walked into the NICU early one morning, just days after HK's birth, one of the nursing staff quietly motioned her to the hallway. Pearl had already noticed more than the usual gaggle of medical staff huddled around HK's crib. The nurse presented her with news she was not prepared to hear—overnight he had developed a bleeder deep within his brain. On a grade of one to four, it was the worst kind, a grade four. At this point surgery was not an option, and there was scant hope he would survive either way, so they bombarded him with antibiotics, scanned his brain multiple times daily, and waited. Pearl hoped and prayed for a good outcome, but raw intuition led her to fear otherwise. Over the next four days, she returned home only to shower and change clothes. On the fifth day head scans revealed that the bleeding had stopped and the volume of blood was starting to dissipate. This time Pearl cashed in a miracle. But years later this stroke-like episode was identified as the likely culprit behind her grandson's paralysis and the underdevelopment of his body's right side, coupled with an eventual diagnosis of cerebral palsy.

Surviving that episode, the premature baby boy displayed unprecedented improvement, allowing doctors, nurses, and Pearl the rare opportunity to exhale, filling the bright hospital room with fragile optimism. With the crisis over, doctors discontinued the steady drip of IV antibiotics. But two days later he descended into severe respiratory distress. Hopes of unfettered improvement faded like a new pair of jeans.

Doctors diagnosed HK with patent ductus arteriosus, or PDA, a life-threatening heart condition and the most common heart problem in premature infants. Pediatric specialists intricately described HK's latest malady as a prenatal passageway failing to close. This condition prevented normal blood flow to his newly developed lungs. Again, all surgical options were off the table, and his survival odds sank with every passing hour.

Doctors restarted the antibiotic drip and moved HK to a

high-oxygen environment, hoping to buy time for his frail body to withstand delicate heart valve surgery. Their gut medical instincts turned him around, and within a month he was strong enough for the operation. Heart surgery proved successful, but doctors later discovered that his monthlong exposure to a high oxygen concentration had caused retinopathy of prematurity (ROP), the abnormal, disorganized growth of fetal blood vessels in the eye, resulting in retinal detachment and blindness.

Pearl finally brought her tiny grandson home on October 11, 1990. Her compassionate gas company supervisor allowed her flexible working hours long before the concept was in vogue. But she still had to work, which meant she desperately needed extra hands to help with the baby. Jimmy, her younger son, had fallen into hauling loads just like his daddy and was constantly on the road driving cross-country. Besides, he saw it as his older brother's responsibility to be at home helping with his infant son. Eventually William landed a decent steady job working for an airport parking company, enabling him to live in Nashville, but he was of little help. His unpredictable rage and bipolar-like personality made him unfit for anything except an occasional diaper change or fetching baby food from the refrigerator. Help and an extra pair of hands finally arrived when Pearl's ailing mother came to Nashville for a week. She ended up staying two years.

CHAPTER 9

Sunday's Child

A month after HK left the hospital, Pearl's life reached a tolerable equilibrium. Still, they were no strangers to the pediatric intensive care unit. HK's weak lungs could not handle bouts of bronchitis, pneumonia, or asthma. During one stretch he would not eat and became weak and jaundiced. After batteries of tests, endocrinologists finally diagnosed a dangerous thyroid deficiency that would require a lifetime of drug therapy. Throughout his extended stay in the NICU, multiple surgeries, follow-up emergency hospitalizations, physical therapy, and intensive counseling, HK received nothing but world-class medical treatment from the extraordinary professionals at the Vanderbilt University Medical Center and Children's Hospital. Quite simply, he would not have survived without their exceptional level of care, and Pearl was profoundly grateful that almost all of his massive medical expenses were covered by government-funded health care programs.

As HK approached eighteen months old, a time when most babies have taken their first awkward steps, he struggled to be mobile, but his paralyzed right side prevented a normal crawl. Undeterred, he compensated by adapting a sideways scoot, like a slithering sidewinder, which seemed to work just fine. Like every other toddler, he moved wherever he wanted, only a little slower and in his own distinctive style.

Scooting on hardwood floors, even a short distance, was tough on his tender skin, so Pearl addressed the problem by creating a four-by-ten-foot playpen. Fashioned from a rubberized exercise mat about two inches thick, it served as a soft cushion and gave him plenty of room to maneuver. She placed three white plastic bins, containing diapers, baby lotion, powder, and other baby supplies, on the floor next to his playpen.

One evening while Pearl and her mother washed the supper dishes together, her mother sensed a desperate need to lighten her daughter's spirits. Among her jewels of wisdom was one that offered a dose of realism mixed with hope: "Life is never as good as it looks or as bad as it seems." Pearl thought that sounded about right. As they talked on, sharing two lifetimes of struggles, they suddenly realized the house had gone unusually quiet.

Terrified of what the tiny baby might have gotten into, the two mothers frantically rushed into the living room. The scene that greeted them was one they would never forget. HK had slithered around the playpen and discovered the mysterious cache inside one of the white plastic bins. Somehow he had managed to open the bin and, to his unfathomable joy, encountered a giant-sized jar of Vaseline.

The sight stopped both women in their tracks. Not only had HK found the Vaseline, but he had somehow managed to pry open the lid and cover himself head to toe in glorious globs of the gooey mess! The unfamiliar sensation must have been especially soothing because his tiny hand had plunged into the jar over and over until it was empty. Mother and daughter began laughing so hard they cried. Any attempt to speak resulted only in more uncontrollable fits of laughter. They sorely needed comic relief, and they got a hefty dose of it that evening. Pearl described the scene to me, saying, "He looked like a large melted candle in the middle of his playpen." Determined to remember the rare happy moments alongside the truckloads of regrets, she used her old Polaroid camera to forever capture the melted candle that for one unforgettable night adorned her living room floor.

Despite such moments of comic relief, life was anything but easy. Pearl's trouble-ridden past—and struggles with not being a morning person—contributed to her belief that the start of a new day never brought anything good. And now her future looked every bit as bleak as her past.

The philosopher Mother Goose described Pearl's future this way:

> *Monday's child is fair of face,*
> *Tuesday's child is full of grace,*
> *Wednesday's child is full of woe,*
> *Thursday's child has far to go,*
> *Friday's child is loving and giving,*
> *Saturday's child works hard for a living,*
> *And the child that is born on the Sabbath day*
> *Is bonny and blithe, and good and gay.*[1]

She explained her take on the little rhyme: "HK is a Sunday's child, and I'm a Wednesday's child. I have to work every day to overcome my tendency toward a negative attitude."

---

1. *PoemShape* (blog), "Monday's Child Is Fair of Face," September 21, 2013, https://poemshape.wordpress.com/2011/01/01/mondays-child-is-fair-of-face/.

And overcome it she did. From HK's first day home, she consciously avoided placing a cold, dark cloud over her grandson. Instead, she opted for the warm sunlight of positive reinforcement and unrelenting encouragement. "Fake it till you make it" became her constant mantra. Every morning she welcomed him with "Good morning! Isn't it a wonderful day?" She manufactured happiness and optimism, even when her world continued crumbling around her.

Pearl managed to struggle through a life she never asked for by facing a future the only way she knew how—one day at a time. And she did it with undaunted courage and determination. A passing inquiry about her day always generated the same standard reply, oozing with a thick slice of unadulterated sarcasm: "Lovely, lovely, lovely!" But Pearl Derryberry carried one genuine trait that required no manufactured facade, no disguised agenda. She had gumption, and she had it in spades.

CHAPTER 10

—✵—

Reality Sets In

As we talked one particular Saturday, Pearl gently lowered her guard and told me a little more about William, HK's father. Though he was worse than useless in caring for his son, he had stayed in Nashville for five years after the accident. "Then," she said, "one cold February morning when HK was five years old, William stopped by the house before heading to work in Columbia. I hate pumping my own gas because the fumes make me sick, so I asked if he would follow me to the Par Mart convenience store just around the corner and put gas in my Toyota pickup. He'd done it occasionally because I'd pay to fill up his old, run-down truck too. He topped off his vehicle after filling mine and then walked around to my window, leaned in, and with a snarky grin on his face, stammered, 'Well, I'll see you later.' We haven't seen or heard anything from him in almost ten years. He truly got the jump-and-run gene from his daddy."

Through the years our restaurant visits also yielded sensitive personal information about her immense struggles and HK's disabilities. By default she had become proficient at managing the countless medical issues that plagued HK, including cerebral palsy, thyroid deficiency, asthma, blindness, seizures, slight brain damage, and limited use of his right arm and hand. His left leg grew one and a half inches longer than his right, which caused a pronounced limp. She lovingly referred to his right arm as "his chicken wing, because when he walks it flops up and down like a bobble-head doll."

Over time Pearl had learned to administer HK's daily prescription regimen, including drugs to maintain thyroid function and control seizures, allergies, and acid reflux. He required two breathing treatments daily to minimize asthma attacks and, at bedtime, gel in both eyes for moisture. He will require a lifetime of caregiver assistance to perform basic daily functions such as toileting, bathing, dressing, eating, and walking. "He would be a handful for anyone," she confided.

Pearl explained the multiple surgeries, some successful and some not, HK had endured since birth. Eye specialists were initially optimistic that his blindness could be corrected through surgery, providing him with limited vision. But the attempts were unsuccessful. And after consultation with world-class eye experts, including Nashville's Dr. Ming Wang, Pearl was presented with the devastating news that the damage was irreversible. HK would be blind for life. Pearl counted his lack of vision as one of her biggest disappointments for HK. "It would make all the difference in the world if he could see just for a minute. How do you explain colors to someone who has never seen them?"

His ongoing medical care included twice-a-week visits to the children's hospital for occupational and physical therapy. And this did not count the occasional emergency room visits for asthma flare-ups or severe colds that could easily degenerate into pneumonia.

———

Pearl also revealed to me the multiple mysteries about his drab attire—which I had noticed rarely changed, regardless of the seasons or outside temperature. His black grandma-looking shoes had bewildered me from the start. She explained in her matter-of-fact style that each of his feet was a different size and so tiny that he could only wear a woman's-sized shoe. The size difference required buying two pairs of shoes at once. She offset the added expense by purchasing herself a pair at the same time and in the same style as his. Thus this shrewd lady snagged a quantity discount with the simultaneous purchase of three matching pairs of women's shoes. Practicality never took a backseat with Pearl. HK wore shorts every day because they slipped on easily over his braces, and the long, white cotton tube socks that stretched almost to his knees protected his tender skin from irritations caused by the braces.

Though the reality of the facts was difficult to process, it all finally made sense. But it still troubled me deeply to think of what they had been through and how they had struggled to maintain even a shade of normalcy.

—∞—

CHAPTER II

Borrowing My Eyes

Increasingly, I became a substantial part of HK and Pearl's social circle. I clearly sensed that she worried about her grandson's future and transition into adolescence. Our tableside conversations were sprinkled with subtle hints of apprehension about the next phase of his life, displaying her deep concern that he had no positive male influences to guide him. At age nine he was emotionally drowning, and I sensed that she was hoping I would become his life preserver. The desperation in her steel-gray eyes pierced me to the core. She seemed to be crying out for help, looking for a mentor, a man to guide her precious grandson along paths she could not travel. Still, I was surprised when one Saturday afternoon she threw out a shockingly unsolicited offer.

"It would be fine with me if you ever wanted to take HK away from the restaurant for a short time. I think he'd really enjoy it as well. I know he's very lonely and bored just sitting here all day."

I jumped on that opportunity like a trout on a mayfly. I turned to HK and said, "Boy, that's great! I can always use a weekend helper!" The smile on his face sealed the deal.

We began exploring the Brentwood area and enjoying time together just doing fun things that men and boys do. On some Saturdays we ordered huge chocolate milk shakes at the local Sonic Drive-In while on other days we shopped at B & C Ace Hardware. He enjoyed "assisting" me with weekend errands that often included grocery shopping, getting an oil change, washing the car, or getting a haircut. It never mattered what we did or where we ended up during those early days together. Everything was new and exciting for this sheltered young boy.

HK relied on me for almost everything, and his safety was paramount in my mind. I used every possible precaution, especially when assisting him as he walked with his halting gait or insisting that he buckle up when riding in my car. He reminded me regularly to fasten our seat belts. Sometimes I wondered if he knew the role that seat belts had played in his mother's fatal car wreck. He always prompted me to buckle up. Who needed an incessantly dinging seat-belt alarm with HK in the car? Once, he leaned toward my face and sternly announced, "Mr. Bradford, click it or ticket!" The Tennessee Highway Patrol would be happy to know that its latest radio public service announcement had been such a big hit, at least with this pint-sized listener.

During excursions away from the restaurant, HK gushed with questions about everything under the sun. I knew little boys were naturally inquisitive, but my nine-year-old blind friend's curiosity was off the charts. Riding down the road, he would constantly ask, "Mr. Bradford, what are we passing? What do you see on both sides of the street?" When I told him the color of his clothes, he enjoyed challenging me with questions, such as, "Mr. Bradford, what does white look like?" Being a sports fanatic, he asked, "Mr. Bradford, will you read me the sports page?" Weeks later he could still recite those articles almost verbatim, but at the time I was having too much fun to give that odd little phenomenon much thought.

I became his play-by-play announcer whenever we attended local sporting events, quietly whispering the on-field action in his ear. We were having the time of our lives. I was his master teacher, and he was my dutiful student. Within months I began to notice fewer questions and more two-way conversations with my small passenger. We were slowly making progress. He wasn't just attempting to make conversation, he was using my eyes to see, and that was just fine with me. He could borrow them anytime.

One weekend I hatched a plan that resulted in a first-time experience for both of us. I knew HK had grown accustomed to the meals at Mrs. Winner's, but I was equally confident that he had not ventured far beyond the typical fast-food type of restaurant. My plan was to expose him to a casual dining experience with a special attraction for kids—something beyond what the major fast-food chains offered. Based on our previous visits to Sonic, I knew he loved chocolate milk shakes. Without knowing exactly why, my mind settled on Steak 'n Shake, the retro '60s-style diner famous for steakburgers and thick, frosty milk shakes made with hand-dipped ice cream. It was an easy fifteen-minute drive down Interstate 65, and I thought it would be the perfect spot to enjoy our first meal away from Mrs. Winner's dining room.

"Have you ever eaten at Steak 'n Shake?" I asked.

"No," he responded matter-of-factly.

"Do you like hamburgers?"

"No, I don't like hamburgers."

Surprised at this response, I asked, "Are you sure you don't like hamburgers? I thought all boys liked hamburgers."

"I'm sure. My Grammy told me I don't like hamburgers."

(Following up later with Pearl, I learned that she had, in fact, told him multiple times that he did not like hamburgers because the tiny food particles from the meat patty would stick between his baby teeth and irritate his gums until she could floss them.)

By this time I had thought so much about enjoying a delicious hamburger at Steak 'n Shake that I was craving one. Not wanting to delay lunch while hunting for another restaurant, I resorted to a bit of shameless subterfuge.

"Have you ever eaten a steakburger?"

"I don't think so."

"Boy, that's great! You don't know what you've been missing. You'll like steak much better than a regular old ground beef burger. It's the most expensive part of a cow."

Even this little blind kid saw through my sloppy sales pitch. He was not totally convinced that any food with burger in its name would soon join his list of favorites. But his face lit up with a striking smile anyway. He was game to give it a try.

As I held his good left hand, we entered the shiny black-and-white-tile restaurant. We were cordially greeted by a high school-aged fellow wearing a spotless white uniform complete with a matching white paper hat folded like the old military-style service cap I had worn many years prior while serving in the army. Our young host directed us to a booth near the back of the restaurant's seating area. We slowly maneuvered to our seats in full view of a packed dining room.

HK's noticeable limp, withered right arm, and hand waving up and down made for quite a spectacle. I remember thinking that we had not attracted this much attention during our other outings. For some reason these particular restaurant customers were glued to us the entire journey. Before meeting HK, I remembered being in their shoes.

Our greeter seated us and handed me two menus. Even before I glanced at the colorful specials, the delicious smell of sizzling steakburgers began to tantalize my taste buds. Probably HK's too. Looking around, I noticed a well-dressed lady staring at us from a table across the dining room. She was about my age and appeared to be enjoying a casual lunch with three others. After watching us navigate through the dining room, her face exhibited the undeniable look of pity.

Our waitress, Evelyn, appeared carrying two glasses of water. Looking directly at me, she asked, "Hon, are you boys ready to order?" Before I could respond, HK replied with an enthusiastic "Yes!" even though we had not had time to discuss the menu. Each of us ordered fully loaded steakburgers complete with fries and large chocolate shakes. At first I was apprehensive about his sandwich choice, given his earlier hamburger comment, but not for long.

Ten minutes later Evelyn delivered our food. I cut his sandwich into four smaller pieces and sat transfixed, watching him devour the steakburger like a famished young tiger cub chomping his first solid food. He ate one hot fry at a time, but only after the steakburger was gone. I quickly concluded that he was a big fan of the more expensive cut of beef. Slowly he moved his fingers side to side across the now-empty plate.

"Mr. Bradford, did I eat it all?"

"You ate everything but the plate."

"Mr. Bradford, you're only joking with me, aren't you? You know I can't eat a plate."

"I'm sure glad because I can't afford to pay for both a plate and a steakburger."

———

As we finished our meal, the female stranger across the dining room shot more probing glances our way. Before we could leave, she stopped at our table, looked directly at me while gently patting HK on the head, and said, "You certainly have a very handsome son."

"Thank you so much. He is very handsome, and I'm very proud of him."

HK burst into laughter as she walked away.

"Mr. Bradford, she thinks I'm your son!"

"If it's okay with you, we'll just keep that our secret. You know I don't have a son."

"That's okay with me, but you know I can't keep secrets."

This offhanded comment should have set off alarm bells inside my head, but I gave it no more thought. Unfortunately, he has reminded me of that admission plenty of times since then!

Later, recalling our unusual encounter, I wondered what thoughts flashed through this total stranger's mind. Was she being genuine or just making small talk because I had caught her obvious stares? Was she being polite, or was that her way of expressing sympathy? Her thoughts probably centered on pity for HK. Perhaps she felt sorry for me as a dad bearing the lifetime burden that rested on my shoulders. In all honesty, before meeting HK, that's exactly what I would have thought.

CHAPTER 12

—ᴍ—

School Challenges

My picture of Pearl and HK's life away from Mrs. Winner's became clearer each time she sat down to talk. I learned that at age three, HK was one of the youngest children ever to attend the Tennessee School for the Blind. Students from across the state, ranging from pre-kindergarten through high school, lived in residential cottages on the school's central campus during the academic year, returning home each weekend. After a few years, Pearl decided that HK would benefit by staying on campus one night a week, even though her house felt lonely without him.

His age and disabilities created major difficulties for the school's highly qualified staff. Given his multitude of physical challenges, the long road from a toddler to a functioning child was littered with obstacles that not even this experienced group of professionals could imagine.

His earliest school years were spent in classes equivalent to a nursery school. For HK, these formative years entailed learning the most basic motor skills, such as crawling, walking, and communicating. His initial educational challenge was learning to read and write braille. Phyllis Alfreda, one of his first teachers and his greatest advocate, tested his aptitude for learning braille at age six. In addition to confirming his aptitude for braille education, her records noted two conclusions: his intelligence quotient tested within the normal range, and he demonstrated an unusual recall of certain things, like his medical history and detailed chart information.

Because he had multiple disabilities, school staff knew it was extremely important to examine each individual limitation. His disabilities were studied and carefully analyzed, both separately and as each interacted with others. Braille proficiency required both hands, and without the use of his right hand, HK faced a monumental hurdle. Swimming against the tide of current practice, Phyllis never let him give up and never wavered in her determination to teach him how to read and write braille. Soon he was practicing with one hand on the keys of a regular two-handed braille machine, but he struggled mightily. In most cases students with multiple disabilities were not taught to read and write, so from the beginning, school administrators had serious doubts about HK's academic abilities.

Only one question hung in the air, and it was huge: Could HK possibly master braille with one hand, a skill that only one other student in the school's 150-year history had accomplished? To do that, he would need a braille machine that operated with just one hand. At that time only one such machine existed. A new one-handed Unimax braille machine cost $700, versus $600 for a regular two-handed machine. It took relentless convincing, but

Phyllis and Pearl doggedly and successfully pursued school admini-strators for funds to purchase the more expensive machine for HK.

Braille lessons kicked into high gear during school hours, but at night he was left without a way to practice his skills. The one-handed braille machine was school property and could not be removed from the classroom. But fate intervened one day while Pearl was getting the oil changed in her truck. It was one of those rare days that she was off work and HK was out of school. Chatting with the service manager at Rivergate Toyota, Pearl shared their dilemma of needing a personal braille machine for HK to use at home. Two weeks later the dealership employees proudly presented Pearl with a check that covered the funds she needed for a new machine. During the previous pay period, they had generously passed the hat to help with the expense. Needless to say, that day Pearl became a loyal Toyota customer for life.

Phyllis Alfreda never wavered in her commitment to provide HK with a learning foundation for life. Working with Phyllis for months both during and after school, and after hours of practice at home with Grammy, HK accomplished the near impossible—he mastered reading and writing words in braille with just one hand. But cross-ing this hurdle did not lessen HK's academic struggles or Pearl's battle with school administrators.

When HK reached his midteens, the annual faculty assessment of his academic progress indicated that he was well below aver-age. Consequently, he was placed in a prevocational curriculum with rudimentary courses that would result in him earning a high school certificate of completion at age twenty-two rather than a normal high school diploma. It was obvious the teaching experts had given up hope that he could conquer a lifetime of intellectual limitations.

But Pearl knew her grandson. In her gut she knew he was a smart student, so she became his biggest advocate and pushed for him to enter a mainstream high school curriculum. Though it was where he needed to be, it was not easy.

Learning wasn't the issue—the challenge was with the various textbooks, such as history and social studies. And it wasn't reading the words in braille with one hand that caused the problems; it was tracking each line or sentence of text that proved nearly impossible. Because single-spaced braille is written tightly together, with each letter consisting of six dots, without a second hand to trace each line of text, HK was simply reading groups of words rather than complete sentences. The school's counseling staff introduced Pearl to a new computerized braille reading device called Braille Lite—a machine that generated one line of braille script at a time. This would solve HK's issue with reading multiple lines of text.

School administrators knew about the latest device, but once again, funding for the expensive machine was not in the budget. Pearl met with the school hierarchy to make her emotional plea for the resources needed to acquire the device. In spite of the 1990 Americans with Disabilities Act (ADA), which mandated reasonable accommodations for people with disabilities, they dug in their heels and stood behind their initial assessment of HK's learning capabilities, doubting the benefits of a Braille Lite machine. Undaunted, Pearl charged ahead and threw down a challenge. "All I ask for is a Braille Lite and a teacher to show him how to use it for the first nine weeks of the school term. If he doesn't make substantial progress by then, he can go back into the prevocational program."

Pearl won this battle, and with assistance from Bill Schenk, another extraordinarily devoted educator, HK began making significant academic improvement. Bill saw in HK what most teachers failed to see. Bill had the patience, the heart, and a genuine passion for teaching, and he volunteered untold hours before, during, and after school to tutor HK in every high school subject. His efforts boosted HK's confidence, which resulted in a remarkable turn-around in his overall academic achievement. Beginning with the 2006–2007 school term, HK, at sixteen years of age, had met all academic requirements to begin seventh grade.

CHAPTER 13

—m—

Brenda's Surprise

Pearl's trust in me grew with every successful trip HK and I took away from her watchful eyes. Before I realized it, twelve months had passed since our first introduction at Mrs. Winner's. We had been to all parts of Williamson County and visited every Brentwood area hardware store, dry cleaners, barbershop, and retail establishment multiple times. We were on a first-name basis with businesspeople all over town. They all got a special kick out of the inquisitive little blind boy. Our friends at Ace Hardware went out of their way to introduce him to customers, let him feel grass seed, touch assorted tools, and operate various machines. They always patiently explained what these things did and answered his multitude of questions. HK is still their most recognized customer even today, with over a dozen photographs of him prominently displayed at the checkout counter.

While we had explored almost every square inch of Brentwood, there was one special place HK had not yet visited: our house. That all changed one Saturday afternoon in December 2000. When I asked if he would like to visit our home, his immediate response was a resounding "Yes!" When I discussed my plan with Pearl, she said, "I think that will be fine. I get off work at seven, so you can bring him back any time before that." Her response excited us both, maybe HK a little more than me.

HK and I left the restaurant that Saturday happily strutting to my car, hand in hand like a two-man marching band. As I drove to our subdivision, I explained my strategy for a surprise: "If you keep real quiet when we arrive, we'll slip into the house and surprise Brenda." In response, he was as quiet as a church mouse.

Turning into our driveway, I again reminded HK, "Don't say anything or make noises when we go in the house. That way we can spring our surprise on her." I re-emphasized my plan because I remembered his earlier disclosure about his inability to keep secrets. I explained how we could quietly ease into the kitchen where Brenda had been baking a four-layer red velvet cake when I left earlier that morning.

Moments later I learned that people with cerebral palsy, especially adventurous kids, can't always control their emotions or fully comprehend the meaning of silence. As I unlocked the rec room door, HK started laughing. And in spite of my repeated warnings, his cackles grew increasingly louder.

"Who's in my house?" Brenda shouted from the kitchen. With that, HK laughed so hard he could barely breathe. His face was now beet red, and he could not walk, even with my assistance. Later I learned that extreme excitement stimulated his cerebral palsy, affecting muscles and causing his upper body to bend almost to knee level. He seemed to be standing in a fetal position, all the while giggling nonstop. I was barely able to keep him from toppling over.

We heard footsteps coming down the hallway, which triggered yet another round of laughter. Brenda suddenly appeared in the doorway and asked, "Who do we have here?"

"Brenda, this is my good friend HK Derryberry," I proudly announced.

"Well, hello, HK," she said.

He caught his breath at last, strained to stand as erect as possible, then slowly inhaled and spoke in a low, almost unrecognizable, squeaky voice.

"What's your name?"

"My name is Brenda, and I've heard a lot about you."

"Who told you about me?"

"Mr. Bradford."

"Brenda, what time did you get up today?"

At that point I intervened and calmly instructed him. "HK, don't give Brenda your second degree. She wants to know more about you and doesn't have much time because she's in the middle of baking a cake." I glanced at her tender smile, and I had a feeling that their bonding process had begun.

When Brenda asked HK about his favorite foods, he informed her that he liked all kinds of food—anything except broccoli. As luck would have it, that green vegetable was prominently featured as part of that night's nutritionally balanced dinner menu. Despite his revelation, she cut several stems of steamed broccoli into bite-sized pieces and put them on his plate. A sampling of other steamed vegetables, along with baked chicken and homemade corn bread, comprised his first meal at our house.

After HK discovered the broccoli pieces, it was obvious that either (a) he was extremely hungry, (b) he had never before eaten broccoli prepared this way, or (c) he was being especially respectful to Brenda during this first visit. We were astonished to watch him devour each piece of broccoli on his plate, along with every-thing else.

"HK, do you want more broccoli?" Brenda asked.

"Yes, Brenda. I didn't know I was eating broccoli. It's really good," he answered through a mouthful of food.

He loved the juicy green florets, like children love chocolate. If the Broccoli Growers Association of America could have seen the way this little fellow devoured their namesake, they would have made him a national spokesperson or their National Broccoli Poster Child, if there were such a thing!

During another dinner experience in our home, Brenda brought out a half gallon of chocolate milk she had purchased especially for HK. I always bought him sweet iced tea at Mrs. Winner's, but we thought chocolate milk would be a healthier substitute. As she poured the cold milk into his plastic cup, complete with lid and straw, she said, "HK, I'll bet you like chocolate milk."

"I don't drink chocolate milk."

"HK, I thought all boys liked chocolate milk."

"Oh, I like it a lot. I just don't drink it because Grammy says it costs too much and we can't afford to buy it."

Brenda looked at me, slowly shaking her head, and continued filling his cup without saying a thing. She placed the full cup of chocolate milk in front of him, and he immediately moved his left hand back and forth until he found it. Gently grasping the cup, his lips found the straw, and he proceeded to drink every drop of chocolate milk without once removing the straw or taking a breath. It sounded like water gurgling down a sink drain. He topped it off with one deeply inhaled suck on the straw that made even more noise.

From that moment, chocolate milk became HK's favorite bever-age choice. We always made sure we had a full half gallon per visit, and before he left, the plastic jug was almost always empty. Our delight in watching him enjoy such a simple gesture was priceless. And, on the practical side, we knew that his maturing bones would benefit from the additional calcium in his diet.

—⁓—

CHAPTER 14

No Tree, No Lights, No Santa

During and after our first dinner together, HK bombarded Brenda with question after question. What did she do all day? Why didn't she work like his grandmother? What were her plans for tomorrow? Why hadn't she visited him at the restaurant? She politely responded to his interrogation, sharing family stories, discussing places we had lived, describing where she grew up, and naming destinations we had visited while on family vacations.

The subject of family vacations sparked an unusual interest from our evening's guest. He sadly shared that he'd never been on a vacation.

"I hope to go to Florida someday. I want to walk on the beach and play in the ocean, which I hear is lots of fun."

"HK, I'll bet you get to go to Florida one day," Brenda responded, never realizing that in a few years she would be the first one to make his dream come true.

The three of us enjoyed our after-dinner conversation so much we completely lost track of time. During one lull in our tableside chat, HK pushed the button on his talking wristwatch. "It's 6:55 p.m.," the watch declared. I suddenly came alert. Pearl's shift ended in five minutes, and I was supposed to have the boy back before she got off work. I immediately called her. Not wanting to start off our first home visit on the wrong foot, I told her we were having so much fun enjoying time together that we hoped she would allow him to stay a bit longer. My offer to bring him home later helped seal the deal.

Soon after Brenda finished kitchen-cleanup duty, we moved our conversation to the den. HK sat on the sofa next to Brenda, holding her hand as they talked for more than two hours. Before I left to take him home, HK hugged Brenda tightly and said, "Brenda, thank you for letting me eat with you and Mr. Bradford. You are the world's best cook, and you make really good broccoli. I love you."

"HK, I love you too," she proclaimed in a voice that betrayed a sizable lump in her throat.

As we left the house, I noticed a familiar twinkle in my wife's eyes. Invisibly, silently, the small pickpocket had struck again, snatching another unsuspecting heart. Our lives would never be the same.

Interstate traffic was heavy for a December Saturday night, no doubt because it was the holiday party season. Pearl had given me detailed directions, but nighttime driving made me naturally cautious, especially since I was venturing into an unfamiliar part of Nashville. HK was not equipped for navigator duties, so I was on my own.

As we approached the East Nashville area where they lived, I noticed scores of cars that had seen better days lined bumper-to-bumper along the street. People milled around in open areas and on front porches of the James A. Cayce Homes, Nashville's largest public housing project. The only warmth came from strings of twinkling Christmas lights lining most of the units.

I clenched the steering wheel tighter and accelerated a tad faster as we drove east through the projects for seven city blocks and then south for six more. Finally I reached Electric Avenue, a street lined with small, 1950s-style wood frame houses. I stopped in front of the only white house without any Christmas decorations—just a brightly lit front porch. I could see no window coverings anywhere as I verified the house number. With the inside lights burning brightly, all I could see were cardboard boxes stacked to the ceiling.

"HK, your Christmas decorations aren't up yet. When does Grammy usually put them out?"

"We don't really have any Christmas decorations. Grammy says they cost too much and they're too much trouble."

"Not even a Christmas tree?"

"No, we've never done that."

"What about Santa Claus? Does he visit your house on Christmas Eve?"

"No, I've never met him."

We got out of the car and walked up the porch steps where Pearl patiently waited. Right away HK began telling her everything about his evening and Brenda's wonderful food. I clumsily expressed appreciation for her understanding, allowing us a longer visit than expected. But the whole time I was looking past her, through the front door and into a living room filled with more boxes but no evidence of furniture or Christmas. My heart sank as I grasped the sad reality. I could think of nothing else during my return trip to Brentwood.

If Brenda had her way, Christmas would be a year-round celebration at the Bradford house. Instead, she settles for the month of December. She starts planning and organizing our sizable assortment

71

THE AWAKENING OF HK DERRYBERRY

of decorations the day after Thanksgiving. With years of collecting, she has lots of them. Typically it takes an entire week and hours of Christmas music to achieve the desired festive transformation.

My major responsibility each year is erecting our nine-foot Christmas tree in the den. The chore of placing wreaths on the outside doors and hanging lights across the front of the house also falls to me, but the end result of our collective efforts always adds more to the holiday atmosphere than a dozen snowfalls.

I returned home that Saturday night anxious to share my news with Brenda.

"You won't believe what I discovered when we pulled into their driveway," I began. "Not only did they not have a tree or any holiday decorations, but HK told me they don't celebrate Christmas and don't exchange gifts."

"You can't be serious," she replied. "Did he sound sad or disappointed that they didn't celebrate Christmas?"

"No, he was just matter-of-fact about it. He said Grammy told him she didn't have money or time for such things every year."

Her final words on the subject were short and to the point. "Well, we'll see about that."

On Sunday afternoon Brenda swung into action and sent me all over town with detailed lists of Christmas paraphernalia to lug home. Within a week she added two more special friends to our list of handpicked and wrapped gifts. She decorated a small Christmas tree for HK that matched the one in our den and surrounded it with presents. A few days before Christmas, we hosted Pearl and HK for a holiday celebration complete with refreshments, fellowship, and presents for both of them.

—✥—

CHAPTER 15

"I Just Know Dates"

HK and I made the four-mile trip from Mrs. Winner's to our house on Harpeth River Drive almost every weekend. Brenda and I anticipated the pure joy he brought with him every time he came. We discovered on these visits that his thirst for knowledge never slowed, and his mind never shifted out of fifth gear except when sleeping.

"Brenda, how long have you lived in this house? Mr. Bradford, where did this (object) come from? What is this? What is it used for?"

During one visit he asked a question that puzzled us both: "Brenda, can I explore your house?" We looked at each other, wondering what "explore" meant to a blind ten-year-old boy.

Brenda hesitantly replied, "Sure, HK, if you'll be careful and let Mr. Bradford help you."

"Brenda, you know I will. I'm always careful."

———

Apparently his definition of *explore* was to move slowly and methodically through every room of the house, gently touching each furniture piece and objects on tables, beds, and the floor. He carefully caressed each item and asked specific questions about it. If he picked up any object, he delicately returned it to its original place before slowly moving his left hand to find the next object.

His exploration began in the den, where he gradually worked his way around the room until he was satisfied that he had inventoried everything. Then he moved into the next room in short, synchronized steps like a small robot. Upon reaching the door frame to the next room, he asked, "Whose room is this?"

"This is our daughter Julie's bedroom."

"I didn't think Julie lived here anymore."

"She doesn't. It's still her room when she comes home to visit."

As before, he used walls and other large pieces of furniture to guide himself as he carefully shuffled around the room's outer edges. He touched every object as though it was a delicate figurine that could be easily shattered without extra-special care.

Convinced that he was sufficiently familiar with Julie's bedroom, he found his way back to the door and turned left down the hallway to the next room. This methodical exploration continued for over an hour until he had covered every square inch of the house. Strangely, he repeated this same routine during each of his next five visits. And since that time, he has never asked to go "exploring" again.

—⚋—

With Brenda now smitten and eagerly awaiting time with HK, our weekend visits expanded to include most Saturday and Sunday afternoons. About thirteen months after my first cup of senior coffee, we began a new and exciting chapter of our expanding friendship. Unlike our connection up to this point, this new chapter built HK's rapport with other adults and children his own age. With Pearl's blessing, HK began attending church with us.

My family had been active members of the Harpeth Hills Church of Christ in Brentwood for more than twenty-three years. Brenda and I were convinced that attending church with us would yield many significant benefits for HK. He would have a special event to anticipate every Sunday instead of his usual eight-hour confinement at the restaurant. Pearl would get a bit of relief from the responsibility of keeping him at work, and we would enjoy having a young person accompany us to church, something we'd missed since our girls had left home. It was a win-win idea that would truly be a unique experience for HK.

When we entered the church auditorium with him that first Sunday morning, Brenda and I felt like aliens from outer space. Every head turned, casting a steady gaze on us and our tottering young guest. Some folks, knowing we didn't yet have grandchildren, gave us looks so curious we could almost see the question marks in their eyes. Others simply gawked at the spectacle of his halting gait.

The young first-time visitor hung on every word uttered during that worship service, absorbing unfamiliar sounds while imagining the peculiar events surrounding him—the singing, the sermon, and the strange voices. He was the perfect gentleman and held my hand most of the time, something he still does today.

One of the closing announcements near the end of the service informed the congregation of an adults-only Christmas brunch to be held the following Sunday after worship. The announcer made it clear that children would attend their regular Sunday school classes while adults would gather for the holiday brunch. Upon hearing this news, HK instantly cocked his head to the right so that his good ear was directed toward the announcer. He did not miss any details.

Later, as we drove out of the parking lot, HK spilled what was on his mind.

"Brenda, can kids attend the brunch next week?" he asked. She glanced at me with a smile as she winked and said, "Well, HK, I think so. Do you like brunches?"

"Yes, Brenda, I just loooove brunches."

"That's fine; you can attend the brunch with us."

"Thank you, Brenda! I just loooove brunches."

He could talk about nothing else for the rest of that day. During his visit on the following Saturday, he constantly told us how much he anticipated the church's holiday brunch. He simply could not say enough about it, although he gave it a valiant try. I think he told Brenda more than ten times how much he appreciated being able to attend the church brunch.

"Brenda, thank you for letting me come to the brunch tomorrow. You know I just loooove brunches."

"HK, you're welcome, and I'm so glad you can go with us. Mr. Bradford will pick you up in the morning at the restaurant, and we'll enjoy the holiday brunch together and—"

"Brenda! Brenda!"

"Yes, HK?"

"Brenda, what's a brunch?"

We looked at each other simultaneously and started howling. He joined in the laughter, even though he had no clue as to the reason for it. Since that experience we have relished many unexpected, untimely, and unintended comments from the once-sheltered young boy. He constantly keeps us in stitches.

—◊—

As the mother of two grown daughters, Brenda has developed an intuitive sixth sense when it comes to children. After a few months of HK sitting through church and Sunday school classes with us, she sprung another fantastic idea: "I think it would be good for him to be in a Sunday school class with other children rather than sitting in a classroom of adults." We thought he should join the third-grade class, so we approached a close family friend and outstanding Sunday school teacher about HK joining her third-grade classroom. "Yes, I'd love to have him," she responded.

This decision seemed like such a wise choice at the time, but our friend soon helped us realize our mistake. HK's limited social and verbal skills had not prepared him for a third-grade class, even at the Tennessee School for the Blind. We never realized that he had not yet progressed to the third-grade level at school, even though he was the same age as his classmates.

The teacher quickly discovered that he was unable to function effectively with his group of Sunday school classmates. They were as unprepared for him as he was for third grade. All his classmates had attended church their entire lives and were knowledgeable of Bible stories and church songs, and most could recite Bible verses. They found it difficult to interact with HK. Like most kids, they stared at him a lot.

After a valiant two-week effort, our friend politely shared her observations and misgivings with Brenda. She offered a ray of hope and gently said, "Don't worry. I know things will work out. We just need to find the right class for him." The following week she discussed his situation with the other elementary Sunday school teachers. Everyone believed first grade would be a perfect match.

———

Bingo! At age ten, HK was four or five years older, but physically smaller, than most of his new classmates. Unlike third graders, these younger kids didn't seem to notice his disabilities. They thought he was pretty cool since he could read braille with his fingers and wore large white plastic braces on his legs. HK, who sensed he knew a little more than the younger children, was thrilled in his new environment and made friends easily. His unique personality began to unfold like a rose in springtime.

—❦—

A year passed, and we had hardly attended a church service without HK. One Sunday morning as he and I slowly walked down a hallway toward the church auditorium, we overheard two adult friends in casual conversation. One man said to the other, "The meeting is scheduled for Thursday, March 12th." Out of the blue HK stopped abruptly, almost causing us to fall. He turned his head toward the man's voice and said, "Mister, March 12th is on a Tuesday." Not fully understanding the unexpected comment and never having met this boy before, he asked, "What did you say?"

"March 12th is on Tuesday, not Thursday," HK replied. "Thursday is the 14th."

"Are you sure?"

"Yes, I am sure."

The man was skeptical. Surely he couldn't have made such a mistake. He pulled out his PalmPilot and scrolled down until he found March 12. Then he exclaimed, "Son, you're absolutely right! It is Tuesday. How did you know that?"

"I don't know how I know. I just know dates."

"That's a pretty good trick."

Both men smiled and shook their heads in amazement. Without

saying a word, HK tugged on my hand, letting me know he was ready to resume our walk. As we left church later that morning, I asked him, "How did you know March 12th was on a Tuesday?"

"I don't know how I know. Grammy says I have a special gift."

"You never told me about your special gift."

"You never asked me."

—ɯ—

"Will You Stay Until I Say My Prayers?"

Not long afterward, Brenda hatched yet another brilliant idea. "I think HK should just stay at our house on Saturday nights." Her rationale was well grounded and similar to the one used to gain Pearl's approval for attending church. With HK staying over on Saturday nights, Pearl would get a much-needed break, I would have a chance to dress him for church, and he would get an extra hour of sleep. Plus, I would be relieved from driving to his Electric Avenue home late on Saturday nights. Brenda bolstered her idea by reminding me that we had three perfectly good bedrooms that were rarely used. It dawned on me as she was crafting her closing argument that Brenda, who only months earlier had cautioned me about becoming overly attached to this special little boy, now enjoyed his company just as much as I did. Or maybe even more.

The following Sunday evening I stood on Pearl's front porch and explained Brenda's idea. I spoke softly, not wanting HK to overhear our conversation in case the answer was no. But from somewhere inside the house, he chimed in with, "Grammy, I would like to spend Saturday night with Mr. Bradford and Brenda."

"Well, I guess that will be fine, but I sure will miss you. This house will be quiet and lonely," she declared.

"Grammy, I'll only be gone one night. You won't miss me, and I'll be fine. It will give you a chance to get some rest. Grammy, I love you."

And the deal was done. Pearl handed him off to us with his doctor's contact information and specific instructions to follow in case he suffered a seizure. His last seizure had been three years ago, at age seven. We equipped our home with a breathing machine and kept ample supplies of his daily medications.

His first overnight visit was a unique experience for all of us. As far as I knew, neither he nor Pearl had attended church regularly, but I was pleased to learn that her routine with HK included a nightly prayer before bedtime. The first time I tucked him into bed, he asked, "Mr. Bradford, will you stay with me until I say my prayers?" Every prayer began the same way. First he prayed for his daddy and asked God to "unshackle" him, a term he'd likely learned from the fiery radio preacher. Then he prayed softly for God to unshackle his grandfather and began a long prayer list that always included Grammy, Brenda, me, and a host of other people whom he had heard were sick or experiencing some difficulty in their lives. His list of names was often so long that he actually fell asleep mouthing his words, but I'm confident God heard every one.

Now, for sixteen years since that first night, my weekend routine has included picking up HK early Saturday morning and returning him home bathed and wearing clean clothes by ten thirty Sunday night. Welcoming a houseguest of any age tends to be awkward at first, especially one who has special needs. Fortunately, HK was an easygoing child, and our weekend transition took little effort. He was readily entertained, listening to music or watching any available sporting event. His favorite pastime was playing dominos and card games with Brenda and me or friends who happened to drop by occasionally.

Bridget's bedroom was slowly transformed into HK's weekend living quarters. Having a room of his own was something he had never experienced at his home in East Nashville. There he shared a bedroom with Pearl, sleeping on a small child's bed in a room with practically no closet or storage space.

Apparently his home bathing routine involved only a washcloth, soap, and a bathroom sink. That was plenty when he was younger, but now his personal-hygiene needs were such that he required a tub and lots of hot water. Bath time followed supper on Saturday nights at our house. He was the most enthusiastic bather I have ever witnessed. Water splashed everywhere, especially when we played bathtub basketball. I always spread out extra towels just to keep the bathroom from flooding. Brenda didn't mind the few extra loads of laundry. Besides, she loved hearing our commotion from the far end of the house and appreciated the squeaky-clean results.

I'd seen HK wear the same shorts, T-shirts, tube socks, and shoes year-round, but now it was time for a change. One thing I've learned during my career in the clothing industry is that high-quality, well-fitting clothes are a genuine game changer for almost everyone. A positive first impression, a healthy self-image, and an aura of pride are just a few of the more tangible benefits that the right wardrobe brings to anyone with the self-respect to care about his or her appearance. For HK, it was more about looking like other boys his age.

Brenda and I discussed HK and his clothing options and decided that he needed clothes suitable for a boy his age. So we went shopping for polo-type shirts, khaki pants, lace-up and Velcro men's shoes, and other accessories, such as belts, socks, and underwear. As he grew, I invested in more formal attire, including a sport coat, dress shirts and pants, shoes, bow ties, and even a tuxedo for the numerous wedding invitations that began arriving in our mail for him.

Finding good-quality clothes was easy; getting them altered to fit HK's malformed body proved both difficult and a bit expensive. The postpartum stroke HK had suffered caused his withered right arm to be considerably shorter than his left arm and his right leg to be shorter than his left leg. His right foot was a size 3 while his left foot was a size 5. Fortunately, I knew an excellent tailor who masterfully modified each clothing item to perfection. Shoes, however, proved to be a unique and more costly problem. Just as Pearl had done, I had to buy two pairs of the exact same shoe for him in different sizes, and the right shoe required a built-up sole to accommodate his shorter right leg.

Seeing the results of his properly fitted clothing was worth it, though. Now he looked like any other well-dressed young boy. In his struggle to break out of a lifetime of isolation, dressing well and looking sharp reinforced his self-confidence and provided him with important emotional comfort.

CHAPTER 17

—☡—

"Don't Worry; Mr. Bradford Is a Good Driver"

Brenda and I cherished our overnight weekends with HK, but sometimes our little visitor altered family plans and caused us to limit long-standing social outings with friends. We included him in many social gatherings, yet there were occasions when we needed adult time with friends, so we reserved most every Friday night for "adult functions." Brenda explained to HK that those were events that children do not attend. This was a new concept to HK, who later commented to her, "I never heard of adult functions until I met you."

On Sunday evenings after church, a group of friends, including HK, usually met for a casual dinner. One particular Sunday night we met at Back Yard Burgers, a drive-through and walk-up hamburger chain. The food order line snaked down the sidewalk as our large group gathered, but the line moved quickly, and we were soon approaching the order window. Before we could say a word, the young cashier peered out the window and said, "Well, hello, HK."

"Hi, what's your name?" HK asked.

"I'm Stacy."

"Are you the same Stacy that used to work with my Grammy at Mrs. Winner's?"

"Why, yes, I am."

With every ounce of sincerity in his small body and the innocence of a child, yet in a voice loud enough to be heard by every person in the parking lot, HK erupted, "Are you Stacy that got fired for smoking marijuana on the job?"

Embarrassed yet truthful, he replied, "Yes, HK, I'm the same Stacy."

"I'm sorry you got fired. I hope you've stopped smoking marijuana."

"Thank you, HK. I've definitely learned my lesson."

Brenda and I looked at each other, each reading the other's mind. *Did he just say what we thought he said?* Others simply turned away to hide their laughter.

—∽—

The last weekend of July 2001 found middle Tennessee sweltering through another hot, humid stretch of summer. Brenda and I had planned to forgo church that Sunday to make our semiannual visit to her widowed aunt who lived in Lenoir City, Tennessee, about a 150-mile drive east of Nashville.

We had struggled the day before with thoughts of HK being left behind on Sunday in a lonely restaurant. We made a pact that if Pearl approved, we would take him with us. So I posed the question to Pearl: "Would you allow HK to accompany us to Lenoir City?" Immediately he chimed in, saying, "Grammy, I want to go. I've never been to Lenoir City." She relented under the double-barreled assault, saying, "Okay, but I sure will miss you, and you'll have to be very careful."

"Grammy, you know I will be careful. And you don't need to worry; Mr. Bradford is a good driver."

The next morning we picked up HK at the restaurant for an early start to a long day. He told Pearl good-bye while she reminded me, "Drive carefully, and take good care of my grandson."

As we settled in for our three-hour interstate road trip, he wasted no time asking where we were and what we were seeing on both sides of the road. After more descriptions of hotels, office buildings, and airport runways than she ever imagined possible, Brenda began to limit her answers mostly to describing houses, barns, animals, trees, and other cars.

We took a short break for restrooms, chocolate milk, sweet iced tea, and coffee at McDonald's in Cookeville, about halfway to our final destination. Not even ten minutes after resuming our drive, HK asked, "Brenda, where are we?"

"The interstate sign says we are coming up on Monterey."

"That's where Byron 'Low Tax' Looper murdered State Senator Tommy Burks."

"What did you say?"

"Monterey is where Byron 'Low Tax' Looper murdered State Senator Tommy Burks in October 1998."

Stunned, neither one of us could think of a thing to say in response. News about the gruesome 1998 murder and Looper's arrest had flashed across Tennessee and the nation, but that was three years ago. Byron Looper, the elected Putnam County tax assessor, had legally changed his middle name to "Low Tax" during his campaign for assessor. He ran for the state senate in 1998 against the incumbent Burks, a popular politician and well-known farmer who had held the position for twenty-eight years. Burks was found murdered during the campaign, and Byron "Low Tax" Looper was convicted of committing the crime. We kept HK's odd bit of trivia in our minds and wondered how he knew such a strange story and remembered it so well.

We started a gradual climb up the Cumberland Plateau, a large, flat-topped tableland that rises more than one thousand feet above the region around it. The plateau is generally considered the dividing line between middle and east Tennessee. We were ten miles west of Crossville, and I was driving sixty-five in the faster left lane behind two eighteen-wheelers when suddenly Brenda screamed, "Jimmy, stop! You're going to hit that truck!"

Without warning, the truck ahead was attempting an emergency stop, with smoke billowing from the rear tires and the dual-wheeled trailer swerving back and forth. I hit my brakes, and all I could think was, *God, please don't let anything happen to HK.*

I managed to stop barely twelve inches from the trailer in front, but the vehicles following us were not so fortunate. Turning around to check on HK, I heard brakes squealing and the sickening sound of metal smashing into metal—and I was helpless. It seemed to happen in slow motion, but in reality it was only a microsecond later when we were violently jarred as the sounds of breaking glass and crunching metal exploded behind us. When the noise ended, our SUV was sandwiched between the vehicle behind and the tractor-trailer in front.

I looked first at Brenda, and other than being doused with iced tea, she appeared to be fine. Turning to the backseat, I asked, "HK, are you okay?" I almost lost it when he did not respond and mightily struggled to get his breath, but he was laughing! I was flabbergasted. Immediately I remembered the day he had first met Brenda and how I discovered that people with cerebral palsy often react the opposite way you would expect in highly charged emotional situations. Finally he said, "I'm okay. What happened?"

While Brenda explained that we had been in an accident, I opened the rear door, unbuckled his seat belt, gave him a reassuring hug, and told him that we were all safe. I checked him thoroughly from head to toe and found nothing worse than a small red spot on his forehead, probably caused by hitting his head on the back of the front seat. He was fine, and his breathing was back to normal, but mine was not. I silently thanked God that we had all escaped unharmed.

With Brenda and HK safe, I turned my attention to the other vehicles around us. I assisted a young mother who had two hysterical children still buckled into their car seats in a Honda minivan behind us. She was dazed but unhurt, and her children were just scared. Their crushed vehicle suffered major damage, so I helped move them to the grassy interstate median.

Traffic on our side of the interstate was at a standstill while cars heading west pulled over to help. Luggage, clothing, and personal items were scattered along the highway for twenty or thirty yards. A canary-yellow Chevy Camaro convertible lay upside down on the highway ahead with no movement or sounds coming from underneath. Later we learned that the driver had lost control, jumped the median, and struck a fully loaded eighteen-wheeler just two vehicles ahead of us. It was a double-fatality car crash. Fearing that an accident of this magnitude might make statewide news, I called Pearl to let her know what had happened. HK and I both assured her that he was safe.

Somewhere in the midst of the highway confusion, emergency crews and highway patrol officers arrived on scene. One unharmed victim of the multiple-vehicle pileup was a veteran female police officer. Though she was not in uniform, within minutes she began using her professional skills to render first aid and direct people back to their cars and out of danger. Even after self-identifying as a police officer, she was forced to take a firm stance with some of the more stubborn victims.

She approached our vehicle while I stood outside checking HK. I explained my concern for him and told her that my young friend was blind, had cerebral palsy, and appeared to have sustained a blow to the head where we could see a small red spot on his forehead.

"Hi, young man," she said confidently. "My name is Nancy. I'm a police officer in Scranton, Pennsylvania. Let me take a look."

"Hello, Nancy. My name is HK. When's your birthday?"

She told him, and he immediately responded that her next birthday would be on a Friday. "Wow!" Nancy said. "How do you know that?"

"I just know."

Nancy felt his head, looked at the red spot, took his pulse, and pronounced him in excellent shape, without injuries.

We learned that Nancy, along with her young niece and nephew, were returning from a family reunion in Mississippi. None of her passengers were injured, and their van was drivable, with nothing worse than minor fender damage. She brought her youthful travelers to meet HK, and in no time they, too, were dazzled by his amazing birth-date skills.

It was clear that the small pickpocket had bagged another unwary victim when, two weeks later, a package for HK arrived at our house from the Scranton Police Department. He was thrilled to find a hand-written note from Nancy, along with a Scranton Police Department polo shirt complete with an embroidered badge and a police ball cap. An official proclamation, signed by the chief of police, naming him an "Honorary Member of the Scranton Police Department" made the surprise parcel even more special.

Three hours after the chain-reaction crash, eastbound interstate traffic finally began moving again. Luckily, our vehicle suffered only minor damage to both bumpers and was completely drivable. It was only later that I noticed the upholstery and headliner had been splattered with coffee and tea.

Brenda called her aunt to explain our unfortunate travel delay. It was midafternoon when we finally arrived at the home of ninety-year-old Leona Shelton. Since she had no children, Brenda was mildly anxious about her reaction to young HK. We recalled how she enjoyed our girls when they were young, but in recent years we had begun to notice that Aunt Leona could be quite difficult at times. We heard that she often complained about misbehaving children at the Baptist church where she had been an active member for more than half a century.

When we introduced HK to the elderly matriarch, he greeted her politely, saying, "It's nice to meet you, Aunt Shelton."

"It's nice to meet you, too, HK. I've heard lots about you from Brenda and Jim," she replied.

"Aunt Shelton, when is your birthday?"

"Honey, I'm so old I don't think you want to know."

It was love at first sight for both the eleven-year-old blind boy and the refined Southern lady. HK hugged her right away, and for the next hour he sat snuggled next to her in the high-backed antique chair that was her customary seat during our visits. I never remembered her sharing it with anyone before—not even with our young daughters.

Until Aunt Leona's death four years later, we made the six-hour round-trip drive to Lenoir City once every three months. Brenda took plenty of pictures each time, sharing precious images of HK with her elderly aunt, many of them sitting together talking. It wasn't unusual to see the framed results prominently displayed throughout the house during our next visit.

A few weeks after her funeral, the attorney for Leona's estate gave Brenda a large box collected from personal effects in her house. It was filled with a lifetime of family photographs, but the ones on top included more than two dozen images of Leona and her new special friend. Frequently we heard him say, "I miss Aunt Shelton. I wish she hadn't died. She was such a nice lady, and I loved her."

CHAPTER 18

—⁓—

Bluegrass and Friends

Nashville is a music lover's paradise. Live music filters out from all kinds of areas and bubbles up in some strange places. In this town, sidewalk serenaders, honky-tonk cover bands, or a baby-faced restaurant server could be the next overnight sensation.

For as long as I can remember, I have been an avid bluegrass music fan. So I was delighted to discover a local bagel shop that has been presenting for several years now a Thursday night live blue-grass show as its way to increase customer traffic. Local pickers and singers combine with a semiregular house band to make a unique experience for the establishment's patrons, complete with bagels and fresh-baked chocolate chip cookies. Our group of friends and Brenda and I are such loyal music lovers that we refer to our outings there as "Thursday night church."

Three years after meeting HK, we started attended the bluegrass church together. I had asked him if he liked bluegrass music, and he had answered exactly as expected: "Yes, I love bluegrass music!"

That summer we became regular churchgoers, rarely missing Thursday night sessions. Normally we arrived no later than 6:00 p.m. to get good seats close to the band and enjoy dinner together. The bagel shop had a combination of round tables and chairs plus a few rectangular farm tables with bench seats on one side and chairs on the other. It was always standing room only.

I took pride in knowing that HK's transformation into an engaging, outgoing personality was now in full bloom, just three years since our first meeting. He seemed to be awakening from a dark place that had been his reality since birth. No longer withdrawn into a lonely shell, with his radiant smile and inquisitive nature, he connected with total strangers like no one I had ever seen. His amazing gift of memory and his day-of-the-week birthday trick immediately captured everyone's attention. Folks who might have started out as strangers quickly became part of his merry band of friends.

Because of the venue's limited seating, we usually shared a table with other bluegrass enthusiasts. As you might expect from this outgoing adolescent, he would always reach with his left arm until he touched the person next to him and say, "Hi, my name is HK. Have I met you before?" No matter the response, his follow-up question was inevitably, "When's your birthday?"

I stayed on guard, listening carefully and prepared to intervene if his tableside conversation went too far. Having personal experience with his endless interrogations, I knew that not everyone would appreciate his unrelenting questions. If I didn't come to their rescue, the conversation might last most of the evening.

One hot July night we made our usual trek to the bagel shop for a dose of bluegrass revival. It was a typical evening with a music-hungry full house. As luck would have it, we had an empty seat at our table. Just before the music started, a young woman scooted into it and, without introducing herself, said, "May I sit with you?"

"Of course, be our guest."

Within seconds HK extended his left arm and started exploring. Reaching as far as possible while moving his arm back and forth, he finally touched her arm.

"Hi, what's your name?" he asked.

"My name is Karen. What's your name?" she whispered, trying not to disturb other listeners.

"I'm HK," he replied, not whispering.

"What's your last name?"

"Lowe."

"Have I met you before?"

"No, I don't think we've met."

"Where do you live?"

I knew immediately where this was going.

"Hi, Karen, I'm Jim," I said apologetically. "HK, Karen is here to listen to music. Let's not ask any more questions right now."

He complied and put a temporary hold on his cross-examination. Looking at his small, inquisitive face, I could tell he yearned to know more about Karen and wouldn't be happy until he did. The bluegrass pickers played for forty-five minutes and then took a short intermission. During the break I usually ordered fresh-baked cookies for the two of us, but tonight HK had another agenda.

We learned right up front that Karen was a reporter for the *Tennessean*, Nashville's daily newspaper. She had come that night to write a feature story about this unusual Thursday night combination of bagels and bluegrass. I'm sure she assumed her assignment would include performer interviews and background material on select audience members. Instead, she found the tables turned: she was the one answering questions and providing background information.

As HK methodically presented each question, Karen politely answered every one. Just as any seasoned reporter, though, she flipped the interview and within no time was the one asking questions.

"Do you like bluegrass music?"

"Yes, I love bluegrass."

"HK, how long have you been a fan?"

"I started coming to bluegrass with Mr. Bradford in June."

With the precision of a skilled journalist, Karen continued her line of questioning during the short intermission, writing his responses in her thick notebook. HK shared an abbreviated version of his life story. He told her about the accident, his mother and father, meeting me in 1999, and the two of us becoming best friends. Karen smiled at his simple yet specific responses and the candor in revealing his most intimate life details. Glancing her way occasionally, I noticed a quivering chin and teary eyes.

After the band's final song, Karen and HK continued their probing conversation outside, where we met her husband patiently waiting to take her home. We exchanged greetings with him and waved good-bye as everyone left the bagel shop. I wondered then if we'd seen the last of Karen. I had a sneaking suspicion that we had not.

I didn't have to wait long for an answer. When we returned to our favorite music venue the following Thursday night, we lucked out and found a table with a bench seat and two straight-backed chairs. As the band tuned up, poised to start at any moment, the familiar brunette with a reporter's notebook appeared.

"Hi, HK. May I join you?"

"Who is it, Mr. Bradford?"

"It's Karen," I said.

"It's nice to see both of you," she replied.

"Hi, Karen, are you the reporter?"

"Yes."

"Why did you come back tonight?"

"I am still working on my article."

Suddenly, HK, for no apparent reason, said, "Karen, I love you."

Caught off guard, Karen paused and replied in a soft voice, "I love you, too, HK."

She explained that she was finalizing her newspaper article, but this time she had a traveling companion assisting her. She introduced us to her photographer, Michelle, who had two expensive cameras slung around her neck and a large black duffel bag full of equipment. Michelle quickly became easy prey for the master. Although Karen had already introduced her associate, HK immediately pounced.

"What's your name?"

"Michelle."

"Have I met you before?"

"I don't think we've met."

"Where do you live?"

Again, I felt compelled to intervene. "HK, don't ask Michelle any more questions. She's here to take pictures and is very busy."

"What is she taking pictures of?"

"Chris, Sally, and other band members."

That explanation must have been sufficient because no more questions arose until the performance ended and we were leaving the restaurant. Just as he had done the week before with Karen, HK quickly turned to Michelle and bombarded her with numerous personal questions about her job, her hometown, even her marital status. He finally asked the date of her birthday, and she was genuinely startled when he told her immediately the day of the week she was born. She informed him she was single, and for a split second I had visions of him asking her out on a date. Much to my relief, that did not happen, and we saw no more of our two journalist friends that summer.

—⚏—

Late one October afternoon Karen surprised me with a phone call at my office. After catching up since our last visit, she laid out the purpose of her call. The tiny pickpocket's magnetic personality and tragic story had snagged two more innocent victims. Just days after our last bluegrass gathering, their newspaper editor had given Karen and Michelle a green light for an in-depth profile on HK and me. The article would be published in the Williamson County section of the *Tennessean*.

"I'm calling to seek your permission to do the article."

"Karen, that sounds great to me," I replied. "However, that's not entirely my decision since it involves HK. I'll need to discuss it with his grandmother. She's a very private person, and I'm not sure how she'll react to such an offer."

Karen understood. "I expected as much. Please tell her we think it will be an outstanding human interest story. We are so impressed with HK. Please try to get her approval."

"I'll call and discuss it with her and let you know what she says. I can't make any guarantees."

"I'll appreciate anything you can do."

I had an uneasy feeling about Pearl's reaction to spotlighting HK's life. Later that evening I called and carefully explained how we met the two journalists at Thursday night bluegrass. I told her about Karen's phone call and her idea for HK's newspaper profile. Thinking it would help secure her permission, I finally said that she would be included in the article.

Somehow I sensed she was cool to the idea before the last word tumbled out of my mouth. Slowly and emphatically, she responded, "I don't think the article is a good idea. It might stir up some ghosts from the past."

I wasn't sure exactly what that meant, but I respected her decision. I didn't question her wisdom or ask any more questions.

"That's fine. I understand. I'll let Karen know."

Slowly I returned the telephone to its cradle, feeling as though the breath had been sucked out of me. My enthusiasm vanished as quickly as it had arisen when Karen made the offer. That night I barely slept at all.

Soon after I arrived at the office the next morning, my phone rang. I dreaded answering it because I knew it had to be Karen. I knew she was excited about doing the HK story and was eager to get started. I picked up the phone, groping for the words to break the bad news to her. Pearl's voice on the line stopped me cold. "Jim, have you spoken with Karen yet?"

"No, not yet. I just arrived at the office a few minutes ago. I plan to call her later this morning. Is there something else you want me to tell her?"

"Well, yes, there is."

She wanted to continue yesterday's conversation, which I had assumed was a closed subject. "After thinking about it overnight," she said, "I've changed my mind. The story is about HK, not about me, and it sounds like a wonderful idea. I know HK will be thrilled. It might even result in something good happening for him. I think it's nice that Karen and Michelle see what we see in him. Please call Karen and tell her that if the offer is still open, she has my consent to write the article."

I was elated, and my enthusiasm returned as though yesterday's conversation with her had never happened. I dialed Karen's number immediately and left a message. Within the hour she returned my call, this time hearing the answer she desperately wanted. She was thrilled.

"I'll coordinate my schedule with Michelle's and call you soon to make preparations for obtaining material we'll need from you, Brenda, Pearl, and HK. It may require spending lots of time with all of you," she warned. I was about to learn more than I ever wanted to know about publishing at a metropolitan newspaper.

Based on discussions with her editor, Karen assumed it would be published in the suburban edition of the daily newspaper. The circulation for the Williamson County edition of the *Tennessean* had a readership approaching thirty thousand. She thought she could have the article ready in two or three weeks.

"Either way, it should be ready in three weeks."

A few weeks passed, then a month, and neither HK nor I heard a word from Karen. Based on stories I've heard about competition for print space, I thought perhaps the whole article idea had been shelved. I never shared these thoughts with HK, knowing that he would be terribly disappointed.

CHAPTER 19

—⁂—

Cover Story

One cold November morning a week before Thanksgiving, Karen called out of the blue to apologize for leaving us hanging. Without giving any details, she explained, "I'm simply waiting on additional input from my editor before launching the project. He seems to have some different ideas than the ones we previously discussed."

These comments naturally aroused my curiosity, but she held her ground. "I can't share details yet. There is something in the wind that could affect the article in a positive way. I'll contact you when I know more."

Great. More time spent waiting and wondering. It was two months into the New Year before I heard any more. Then early one Tuesday morning in February, Karen called my office just as I arrived. I recognized her voice, but it was at least an octave higher than I remembered.

"My editor thinks the initial outline contains such a unique human interest story and HK is so special that he has given Michelle and me approval to write a much larger article, complete with photographs. Naturally, he will have the final approval for the exact content and size of the article."

My pulse quickened as she carefully described the newspaper's latest publication plan for HK's article. His narrative would now be the cover story for *Life*, a multipage magazine insert in the Sunday edition of the *Tennessean*, with a circulation exceeding one million readers.

"This is the greatest opportunity I've had in my newspaper career so far!" Her elation came across loud and clear, and it immediately infected me with the same enthusiasm.

"Congratulations! It sounds very exciting." Now it was my voice that high-jumped an octave. "I know HK will be thrilled. He and I look forward to spending time with you and Michelle."

Karen mentioned that developing our story would require spending lots of time with us, but we were not prepared for the hours upon hours that would be needed to produce the enhanced profile piece. They followed us almost every weekend for four months, gathering in-depth information, conducting interviews, and snapping pictures of Pearl, Brenda, HK, and me. The two reporters became our weekend shadows, following us virtually everywhere we traveled. Karen scribbled enough notes to fill at least a dozen of the four-by-eight-inch reporter's notepads, while Michelle took thousands of pictures from every conceivable angle on her fancy digital camera.

Occasionally our sizable entourage caused a mild furor around Brentwood, and HK loved it. Once, while the journalists recorded us eating breakfast at the local Waffle House, we noticed other customers around us trying hard not to stare and whisper. They were convinced that the little boy with disabilities at the center of attention must be a child celebrity. This was confirmed when just the two of us returned to Waffle House a few weeks later. One waitress told HK that some customers that day thought he was a child actor working on a television movie in Nashville.

"I overheard one lady even say she'd read about the movie in the local paper."

"Mr. Bradford, I'm famous! I didn't know they were making a movie about me!"

I worked hard to explain that there was no movie, just an upcoming newspaper article. Little did he realize that notoriety and fame were just around the corner, but there were still substantial bumps in the road ahead.

Regardless of where we visited with the journalists in tow, everyone knew HK. He was on a first-name basis with practically every employee of Brentwood's many retail establishments. People seemed drawn to his effervescent personality like a bee to a flower. His quirky skill with dates endeared him to others; he was simply remarkable in so many ways. Slowly, steadily, his improving self-confidence began replacing his lonely, isolated world.

It was during this heady time of excitement over the anticipated newspaper story that Pearl was presented news she did not want to hear. HK had just completed his annual medical checkup, and doctors were pleased that it had been more than five years since he had experienced any seizures. His overall health had steadily improved, and his growth, while slower than that of most twelve-year-olds, was progressing normally in all but one area.

The effects of cerebral palsy on his maturing leg muscles were becoming quite severe as he grew toward adolescence. We could actually see the evidence of the problem in his worsening posture.

The curvature of his spine was also more pronounced, causing him to develop a severe stoop. His leg muscles pulled him radically forward when he walked, as though he was about to fall forward at any moment. Doctors told Pearl that he needed corrective leg surgery to release his constricted hamstring muscles. They explained that without surgery, his leg muscles would tighten with age and drastically limit his mobility. He would eventually face life confined to a wheelchair.

This surgery involved a delicate process of separation, stretching, and then reattaching each hamstring muscle. The surgical team at Vanderbilt had extensive experience with this type of procedure, but not on a youngster of HK's age or with his medical history. Under normal circumstances, recovery time was four to six weeks. HK would need longer. Pearl grappled with the decision, but not for long. The last thing she wanted was a wheelchair life sentence for her precious grandson.

The surgery was scheduled for June 2, 2003, after the school term ended. Doctors were optimistic that if everything went well, HK would be able to start school in the fall. The week before surgery I decided both of us needed a healthy dose of Thursday night church, so we claimed our regular pew and settled in for an evening of bagels and bluegrass.

I had told our bluegrass buddies about HK's imminent surgery, and they were ready with encouragement. But all HK wanted to talk about was his emerging celebrity status. Everyone around our table got an earful during breaks in the music. Later that night some of his closest friends presented him with a surprise package. As a crowd surrounded our table, I helped as he unwrapped the gift during one of the breaks. It was a white cotton T-shirt with HOLLYWOOD KID displayed in large gold letters on the front and a big black Cadillac limousine on the back. He was thrilled, thinking it confirmed his importance as a celebrity. But I knew it was just another innocent way to spoil him.

—◊—

Pearl, Brenda, and I checked in HK at the hospital early on Monday morning a week later, almost a month before his thirteenth birthday. His surgery began a little before nine, and nurses told us to expect it to last three hours.

By midmorning the surgical waiting room was teeming with families anxiously awaiting news about loved ones. Several of HK's church friends had come to join us in our vigil. After two and a half hours, a surgery team doctor came in and told us that the operation was finished and completely successful. HK was in recovery while awaiting an open patient room.

Around noon we were told that he had been moved to a regular room but was still heavily sedated and would probably sleep through the afternoon. Brenda, Pearl, and I gathered our assorted belongings and hurried to his bedside. When we entered his room, he was sleeping peacefully with both legs in full casts from the bottom of his feet to the top of his thighs.

It had been a stressful morning and a long stretch since breakfast, so I headed to a nearby restaurant for take-out food. While I was gone, the chief surgeon came in to give Pearl a detailed update. He explained that the procedure had gone as planned with no surprises. HK's prognosis looked good, but the next twenty-four hours would be extremely painful for him. He was heavily sedated and would likely require additional pain medication.

Before leaving the room, the doctor showed Pearl and Brenda the extra cast buildup on the bottom of his shorter right leg. Until both casts came off in about three weeks, the built-up cast would allow him to stand. "But," the doctor firmly told Pearl, "he is not yet ready to stand. Do not get him out of bed for any reason whatsoever without assistance from the nursing staff."

When I returned to the hospital with two bags of food, Brenda was waiting outside HK's room, sobbing uncontrollably.

My heart sank. "What in the world happened?" I cried.

Between tears she explained that Pearl, against the doctor's explicit orders, had gotten HK out of bed and made him stand on his new casts. He was screaming in excruciating pain.

As I passed into his chamber of agony, a pale, wide-eyed Pearl looked up at me and offered a contrite explanation. "I think I did something I shouldn't have done. I got HK out of bed and made him stand up."

"Why?" I was incredulous.

"The built-up part of the cast didn't look right. I wanted to make sure he could stand on it."

HK was still whimpering, and my heart was breaking. Other than that day years ago when I had told him good-bye, causing his meltdown at Mrs. Winner's, this was the only other time I have ever seen him cry. His heart was hurting that time; his legs were in pain now.

Later that afternoon some friends arranged a surprise visit from a local television weatherman who was one of HK's favorite TV personalities. On his way to the television station, the weatherman stopped in to visit and wish the little patient a speedy recovery. Groggy and heavily sedated, HK immediately recognized his familiar voice and muttered, "Thank you for coming to see me. You are my favorite weatherman. I will stay awake to watch your forecast tonight."

The gentleman smiled and replied, "HK, it's my pleasure. I'll send you a special message during tonight's weather segment. I hope you get well soon."

Sure enough, the weatherman kept his promise, and so did HK— with a little help. He was just barely conscious when the ten o'clock newscast began. I had to constantly work to keep him awake for the upcoming weather segment. Finally, he held on just long enough to hear these words near the end of the weather forecast: "My little buddy HK is recuperating from surgery at Vanderbilt University Medical Center tonight. Please keep him in your prayers." I looked over to see his reaction, and he was smiling peacefully, already in dreamland.

A few Sundays later, on July 13, 2003, the lengthy cover story titled "Like a Father, Like a Son" finally appeared in the *Life* magazine section of the *Tennessean*. As if on cue, the telephone rang early that morning. It was Brenda calling from Atlanta, where she was on a weekend business trip. She was eager to hear if the Sunday paper had arrived and whether I had read the article.

"I just finished reading it, and I think it's great," I replied. "I've got tears in my eyes. They did a wonderful job."

She knew HK would be excited when I read him the article and described the touching photographs that captured the essence of our special story. "Please tell HK I am very proud of him."

In the quietness of our empty house, I sipped my morning coffee and slowly digested the article again, this time savoring every eloquent phrase and descriptive detail that our journalist friends had used to communicate our passionate tale. In the sports world HK would be called a champion. Our friends were beginning to see him as a celebrity. But I knew he was a miracle.

CHAPTER 20

—ᕗ—

"You Know, I'm Famous"

The swirling whirlwind of fame caught us all by surprise, especially HK. Having his life story read by more than a million people raised his profile and made us even more visible everywhere we went. People at church rushed to greet us that Sunday morning when the story appeared. They could not wait to tell HK they had read about him in the newspaper. Even our minister told the assembled worshipers to read the article about "one of our most famous members."

It did not take long for the first hints of HK's newfound fame to become full-fledged realities. He was invited to appear on *Talk of the Town*, the local CBS affiliate's noon talk show, then hosted by Harry Chapman. Live television seemed to help the interviewer and his subject bond quickly as Harry walked HK through a series of questions about the article, our friendship, and some of his life-changing experiences. HK carefully answered every question, often pausing thoughtfully before speaking. But with the irrepressible HK on the set, the apparent normalcy of the talk show was not to last.

As he wrapped up the interview, Harry started narrating a live television commercial using a teleprompter. Suddenly HK interrupted him with an urgent request. From off camera, he asked, "Harry, Harry, is Ron the weatherman at the station today?"

"HK, I don't think Ron arrives until around two o'clock."

"Well, will you tell him I said hello when he arrives? He's my good friend."

"I'll certainly do that, HK, but now I've got to finish this commercial."

Cameramen and technicians on the set strained to suppress their wild laughter as the innocent little blind boy momentarily knocked Harry, the consummate television anchorman, off his game. Meanwhile, the teleprompter never slowed during the interruption. Unable to find his place in the commercial, Harry was forced to ad-lib the remainder of the advertiser's copy, once again displaying his seasoned poise and professionalism.

After I left the television studio, my plans were to drop HK off with Pearl, but my cell phone rang before I could drive out of the station's downtown parking lot. At first I thought someone was playing a practical joke on me as the caller introduced herself as a reporter from the local NBC television affiliate. Ironically, while we sat in her competitor's parking lot, she was contacting us to extend an invitation to appear in a local television segment called "Unsung Heroes."

Unlike the live on-air interview, "Unsung Heroes" was a short, prerecorded human interest segment that aired each Thursday night during the six o'clock news and on weekends. This reporter told me she had seen our story in the newspaper, and she assured me emphatically that she had no idea he had just appeared on *Talk of the Town*.

HK, Pearl, Brenda, and I spent hours being interviewed as the reporter gathered information for the mini-documentary. Her camera crew spent days shooting video at some of our familiar Brentwood hangouts. Although produced in a different medium than the print cover story, "Unsung Heroes" also chronicled our unlikely meeting and journey together.

Being featured in a widely read newspaper and on two television stations certainly qualified HK as a local celebrity, and he loved every second of it. Two of our favorite restaurants displayed framed autographed pictures of him next to their collection of famous country music stars. Even though it's been many years now since the cover story first appeared, strangers who remember reading it still recognize him. It's not unusual for people of all ages to approach us today while we're shopping or eating. Typically, these exchanges go something like this:

"Please excuse me, but aren't you that little boy I read about in the newspaper some years ago?"

"Yes. My name is HK. Have I met you before? What's your name? When's your birthday?"

Four months after surgery, while recuperating at our house, HK was shocked one day when country superstar Alan Jackson's executive assistant called to invite us to be his special Grand Ole Opry guests the following week. Thanks to thoughtful friends who knew this assistant, they had planned the royal treatment usually reserved for Mr. Jackson's family members, including a tour of his private bus and backstage seats at the Opry. This news helped kick HK's recovery into high gear.

Arriving at the Grand Ole Opry that special night, our entourage was greeted by a congenial security guard with a clipboard.

After carefully reviewing his guest list and satisfying himself that we were indeed the HK Derryberry party we claimed to be, he said, "Mr. Jackson is waiting to meet you. I hope you enjoy your visit to the Opry." He directed us to a parking lot specifically reserved for Opry performers. I distinctly remember praying that Country Music Hall of Famer "Whispering Bill" Anderson wasn't scheduled to perform that night, because we parked in his reserved spot.

Due to his surgery, HK was temporarily confined to a wheelchair. But that presented no problem because Alan and his assistant had made all the necessary arrangements, including help in transferring his special guest into the bus. I'm sure that Alan's business associate never dreamed his job description included these kinds of tasks, but he performed it admirably, gently seating HK on a small sofa inside the luxurious motor coach.

Shortly after we were seated, Alan and Denise Jackson emerged from their private quarters and warmly greeted each of us. Wearing his trademark cowboy hat, denim shorts, and a T-shirt, he focused in on HK.

"Hi, HK. I'm Alan Jackson, and it's very nice to meet you. I've heard that you're a very special person and one of my biggest fans."

"Hi, Alan. I'm HK, and it's nice to meet you too."

While talking, HK instinctively felt Alan's leg, something he does with most men to see whether they're wearing long pants or shorts, which HK was wearing that night. Realizing that Alan was also in shorts, he said, "I thought you wore long pants with holes in the knee!"

"I'm just relaxing and wearing shorts like you. I'll change clothes before I perform tonight."

"What songs are you going to sing tonight?"

"HK, I'm not sure, but I'll decide before I go onstage."

"Why don't you sing your big hit 'It's Five O'Clock Somewhere'?"

"You know, I might just do that."

"Alan, are you going to tell the audience that I'm here tonight? You know, I'm famous." Everyone laughed, including Alan.

"HK, you know, I might just do that too."

The Jacksons were so warm and gracious that we visited with them for more than an hour. Denise used Brenda's digital camera to take a group shot, a photo that constantly reminds us of that special evening and one that remains prominently displayed on our refrigerator today.

After HK was transferred back to his wheelchair, we were directed through Opry House security to a special audience section onstage directly behind the house band. It was like having a 50-yard-line seat for the Super Bowl. After performances by Porter Wagner, Little Jimmy Dickens, the Whites, Vince Gill, and Steve Warner, our new friend Alan Jackson casually strolled onstage to a rowdy welcome from his loyal fans. Wearing jeans with holes in both knees, Alan began to belt out his hit "It's Five O'Clock Somewhere," much to his special guest's delight. With the final notes still ringing in our ears, Alan dedicated this song to his famous friend HK, who was visiting backstage. I'm confident that HK has this exclusive, once-in-a-lifetime memory tucked away for permanent safekeeping.

CHAPTER 21

The World's Best Blind Pilot

Looking back now, I can see that 2003 marked a turning point for HK and me. My new best friend turned thirteen that year and began experiencing the fullness of life in ways I never could have imagined when I was that age. Even though he was now a teenager, he looked much younger. People sometimes patted his head and spoke to him as if he were a small child, but that didn't seem to bother him. His personality overflowed with curiosity and wonder, always ready for a new challenge.

Becoming a teenager was a big deal for HK, especially when Brenda pulled out all the stops. She planned an extra-special birthday bash with friends and family at one of his favorite Brentwood restaurants. She spread the word that gifts were optional, but she asked everyone to bring a funny birthday card. Oh, how HK loved greeting cards!

Hunting for the perfect birthday card was near the top of his favorite shopping experiences. We could spend hours in our local Hallmark card shop and return the following weekend to scour for fresh inventory. Even then, his quest to find just the right message for a special person often consumed thirty minutes or more, as I read aloud verse after verse from just one section of the latest arrivals. He loved the music-playing varieties, but his main quest was for the perfect card, usually the one that made him laugh the most.

After making the perfect selection, our next hurdle was keeping him from telling the intended recipient, usually Grammy or a friend from church. He simply could not keep secrets. Most of the time the person knew weeks in advance that he or she would be receiving a greeting card and usually knew the exact message contained inside. HK always justified "spilling the beans" this way: "They just really need to know they are getting a card. Waiting for that special day is just too hard."

The first weekend in July found Pearl, Brenda, me, and twelve of HK's closest friends gathered for his thirteenth birthday celebration. One of them came with a special handmade card containing a surprise gift that left the birthday boy speechless. Grand Rivers, Kentucky (population 343), is home to Patty's 1880's Settlement, an award-winning tourist restaurant set on the western Kentucky shores of Land Between the Lakes National Recreation Area, about 115 miles northwest of Nashville. And Gary Waller thought that a visit to Patty's would make the perfect birthday gift for a newly minted teenager, especially if it involved his first airplane flight.

Because HK was still recuperating from leg surgery, the birthday trip had to be postponed almost four months. But on a clear, frosty Saturday morning in late October, the time finally arrived for his long-awaited airplane adventure. It was a gorgeous autumn morning, sunny, without a hint of clouds in sight. Trees showcased their finest colors in shades of burnt orange, golden yellow, and fire-engine red. Winds remained calm, and even though there had been heavy frost the night before, temperatures were predicted to climb into the low sixties later that afternoon. It was a perfect day for flying.

Gary, his brother-in-law, pilot and airplane owner Chris Peugeot, HK, and I met at the John C. Tune Airport—a small general aviation airport located about eight miles west of downtown Nashville, catering mostly to corporate and private aircraft. The cold morning air—thirty-eight degrees, according to a nearby bank sign—gave us all a shiver as we left the comfort of our warm cars.

Chris was deep into his preflight checklist when we arrived. He had moved the single-engine airplane from the hangar and topped off the fuel tank. As we approached the small craft, I had serious doubts that four grown men and a teenager would fit comfortably in the tiny passenger compartment. But our experienced pilot seated us with room to spare. Chris took the left front seat—the pilot's seat; I firmly buckled HK in the right front copilot seat; and Gary and I took the seats directly behind them, leaving his brother-in-law alone in the rear seat.

Before firing up the engine, Chris explained to HK exactly what to expect. He then took HK's left hand and carefully guided it over every gauge and toggle switch, patiently describing their functions while allowing him to feel and understand the importance each one would play in today's safe flight. HK grew intensely serious. I wondered if he felt any fear rising from deep inside.

Chris then carefully placed the copilot's headset over HK's ears. The large black headphones engulfed both sides of his face. His small head looked like the filling between two sides of a giant Oreo cookie. Chris explained the operation of the headphones and told his copilot that he'd be able to hear the air traffic controllers at Nashville International Airport some fifteen miles away.

———

"I will be the only one able to talk with them," he explained. "You'll talk to me during the flight."

Finally, with the faint hint of a smile, Chris explained to HK that if something prevented him, the pilot, from completing the flight, then it would be the copilot's responsibility to get everyone safely on the ground. HK listened intently to Chris's final instructions without uttering a word. After the brief orientation ended, Chris asked, "HK, do you think you can be a good copilot and fly the plane safely?"

"Yes, I know I can. I'm the world's best blind pilot," he calmly replied.

The small plane shook and rattled as Chris fired up the engine. A puff of white smoke rose from under the front cowling. The engine ran smoother after idling a few minutes, and—most important to me—the smoke disappeared. Chris carefully ran through his checklist one last time as an additional safety precaution, and we were finally ready to take to the air.

"We're ready for liftoff. HK, are you ready?" he asked.

"I'm ready!"

Chris taxied onto the runway, gave the engine full throttle, and the wheels soon lifted from the ground as we soared into the sky.

The plane climbed north, giving everyone but our copilot a picture-perfect view of the distinctive Nashville skyline ten miles away. The unmistakable twin spires of the metallic AT&T skyscraper, the "Batman Building," glistened in the crisp morning air like flashing beacons guiding visitors to Music City. We soon leveled off at thirty-five hundred feet, and the colorful foliage of the autumnal countryside took my breath away.

As we settled into the flight, I looked at HK to see if he had taken up the rocking movement that often overtook him when he was excited. Not a wobble. He was as solid as Gibraltar, fully engaged in his copilot's duties, listening to the headphone chatter, and keeping as quiet as a mouse on Christmas Eve. As I studied him, I tried to imagine the thoughts that must have been running through his mind. I distinctly remember wondering if God had somehow allowed him to visualize Earth's majestic beauty below and the enormity of the heavens above.

Chris kept receiving instructions from Nashville approach control until we cleared Nashville air space. Then we were on our own, flying under visual flight rules and Chris calling the shots. After we had reached our chosen altitude and destination heading, he said to his copilot, "HK, are you ready to fly us to Kentucky?"

"Yes, I'm ready!"

After giving him a few more instructions, Chris said, "HK, you're now our pilot."

We never really knew whether the copilot controlled the airplane or not, but HK took on his responsibility with utmost seriousness. He gripped the plane's yoke so hard his knuckles turned white and his body stiffened. He was spellbound, seeming to peer out the cockpit window as though looking for anything that might interfere with our safe journey northward.

An hour later we were closing in on our small Kentucky airport. The copilot relinquished the controls as Chris contacted the airport, alerting them of our pending arrival. I felt pretty sure that the tense copilot welcomed the break, since his hands were undoubtedly sore from maintaining his death grip on the airplane's controls.

Chris taxied us onto a large aircraft parking area, eventually settling next to a larger red-and-white plane. He shut down the engine, turned to HK, and said, "Did you enjoy your flight?"

"Yes. I did a good job flying the plane, didn't I?"

"Perfect! You did a great job getting us here."

A short, portly man, neatly attired in Western wear, approached as our group of air travelers entered the small terminal. His coal-black hair, with hints of gray on the sides, was swept back and glistened as if wet from liberally applied styling gel. He wore a white Western-cut cotton shirt with fancy buttons, heavily starched Levi straight-leg jeans with unbroken creases down the front, and navy cowboy boots with a small piece of ornate silver on each tip. He looked like a rodeo star a few years past his prime. The only thing missing was a ten-gallon hat.

"Is this the HK Derryberry birthday party?" the man asked.

"Yes, I'm HK, and it's my birthday."

"Nice to meet you, HK. I'm Harold. I'm going to drive you to Patty's."

"Nice to meet you, too, Harold. When's your birthday?"

"September 12, 1957."

"You were born on a Thursday."

"Are you kidding me?"

Everyone climbed into the back two seats of Harold's large, highly polished GMC Yukon, and we began the ten-minute ride to Patty's, a century-old landmark restaurant famous for its thick pork chops and homemade bread baked in what looked like small flower-pots. The vehicle eventually came to a slow stop directly in front of the restaurant. Harold turned to the guest of honor and said, "HK, make sure you have dessert. They are out of this world."

"I will, Harold. Thank you for the ride."

A smiling hostess in a colorful floral dress greeted us as we entered the restaurant. She took one look at HK and said, "You must be the birthday boy."

"Yes, my name is HK. Have I met you before?"

"Sugar, I don't think so."

"What's your name?"

"Honey, my name is Barbara."

HK's elementary school photos (*left to right*: ages 6, 8, and 11)

The first photo Mr. Bradford took of nine-year-old HK soon after they met at Mrs. Winner's in 1999

HK using his braille writer to complete his homework, 2001

HK opening his present during a Christmas party at the Bradfords', Sunday, December 22, 2002

Mrs. Bradford and HK keeping warm on a wintry day in December 2000

Photo by Michelle Morrow

Left to right: Herb Shumaker, Jim Bradford, Chris Peugeot (pilot), HK (copilot), and Gary Waller prior to their flight to Land Between the Lakes, KY

Gary Waller and HK performing a preflight check before takeoff, Saturday, October 18, 2003

HK on his first visit with Leona Shelton, Mrs. Bradford's 93-year-old aunt, Sunday, July 29, 2001

Mr. Bradford with his grandchildren, Mac and Catherine, and HK at the church Christmas brunch, Sunday, December 23, 2007

HK navigating the Bradfords' pontoon boat for the first time, Tims Ford Lake, TN, Sunday, May 13, 2001

HK in a competitive Saddle Up horse show, Saturday, April 23, 2005

HK and Mr. Bradford after a highly competitive miniature golf match, Destin, FL, Wednesday, August 9, 2006

Former University of Alabama head football coach Gene Stallings and HK, Sunday, January 4, 2009

Coach Stallings with HK and Brenda and Jim Bradford, Montgomery Bell Academy, Wednesday, August 19, 2009

HK and Mr. Bradford after speaking at Ensworth High School, Monday, April 30, 2012

HK with friends Caroline Solomon (*left*) and Amanda Gonzalez (*right*) at Furman University, Greenville, SC, where he received honorary membership into the Psychology Club, Friday, March 20, 2015

Left to right: Stu and Dot Brandt, Brenda and Jim Bradford, and HK enjoying a seafood dinner, Destin, FL, Monday, August 13, 2012

HK and Brooke Sage dancing at the Tennessee School for the Blind's junior-senior prom, Thursday, May 24, 2012

HK receiving his high school diploma, Friday, June 1, 2012

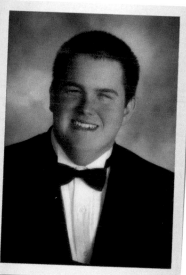

HK with his grandmother, Pearl, during junior-senior prom activities

HK's high school 2012 senior class photo

Former Tennessee Titans head coach Jeff Fisher teaching HK the proper techniques for throwing a pass, Tuesday, January 2, 2001

HK and former Titans All-Pro center Kevin Mawae, Saturday, October 21, 2006

Former Titans All-Pro running back Eddie George and HK, Saturday, July 27, 2013

HK and Chick-fil-A Chairman and CEO Dan T. Cathy, Wednesday, August 20, 2014

Toronto Blue Jays pitcher and former Cy Young Award–winner R. A. Dickey and HK, Saturday, September 14, 2013

HK, now an experienced navigator, on Tims Ford Lake, Monday, June 29, 2015

HK at the desk of the late S. Truett Cathy, during a visit to Chick-fil-A headquarters, Atlanta, GA, Monday, October 13, 2014

Left to right: HK; Sharolyn Snyder; Mike Boyd and his caregiver, Tressa; and Brent Snyder departing from Nashville International Airport for a week of snow skiing in Denver, CO, Monday, January 25, 2016

Mr. Bradford and HK
enjoying a meal at their
favorite Chick-fil-A
restaurant, Brentwood, TN,
Thursday, April 12, 2012

Aly Perry, a Chick-fil-A restaurant manager,
and HK, Thursday, April 7, 2016

Pearl and HK sharing a special moment
during a photo shoot for the *Vanderbilt
Medicine* article, Monday, May 14, 2012

Mr. Bradford and HK enjoying a
beautiful early spring afternoon,
Thursday, March 6, 2014

Photo by Michelle Morrow

"Barbara, when's your birthday?"

Looking sternly at Gary and me, she reluctantly replied, "March 20, 1948." Then HK performed his customary trick and told her she was born on a Saturday. "Honey, I'm amazed," she muttered.

She escorted our small group to a private back corner location. After seating us, she gently touched HK's good arm and said, "HK, I am so proud to meet you. I hope you have a wonderful birthday."

Minutes later our waitress arrived and introduced herself.

"Who's celebrating a birthday?"

"I'm HK, and it's my birthday party. Have I met you before?"

"No, I don't think we've met before."

"When's your birthday?"

She told him, and he immediately responded, "You were born on a Friday."

"Hon, that's impressive. Is it the truth?" she questioned.

Simultaneously everyone at the table replied, "Yes, he's never wrong."

She left momentarily but soon returned with several coworkers eager to meet HK. He told each of them the weekday of their next birthdays, the days of the week they were born on, and even informed one lady that the University of Kentucky Wildcats basketball team beat the University of Tennessee on her birthday in 1995. They all left smiling and shaking their heads in wonder.

Our waitress recommended the best meal in the house, and we all agreed to follow her suggestion explicitly. With five identical orders of Patty's specialty dish—a twelve-ounce pork chop, house salad, and baked potato—she headed to the kitchen. Moments later the mouthwatering homemade bread arrived in the restaurant's trademark flowerpot container. "Are there any flowers in the bread?" HK asked with a laugh.

The birthday meal exceeded all our wildest expectations. It

might have been HK's first time eating an entire pork chop, at least one so large. As usual, he ate every bite and finished by rubbing his fingers side to side across the empty plate, making sure not a single morsel remained.

After everyone finished, our server cleared the table and disappeared into the kitchen. Desserts were never mentioned, but she returned with a thick slice of birthday cake so large it covered an entire dinner plate. The cake had a chunky chocolate crust with coffee ice cream, nuts, caramel, whipped topping, and a big red cherry on top. A single birthday candle was carefully placed in the middle.

She left five forks and extra plates, and soon her fellow restaurant workers joined in a strictly Southern version of "Happy Birthday." With a little help HK blew out the candle, and every man sampled a small piece of the decadent dessert. HK finished the rest.

We thanked our server for her excellent service, and as we left the restaurant, HK told the entire waitstaff that he enjoyed his food and he hoped everyone had a blessed day.

"You ladies don't look a day over eighteen," he deadpanned.

Harold and his big Yukon were waiting out front to return us to the airport. We departed Kentucky that afternoon the same way we had left Nashville earlier that morning. After getting us airborne and climbing to our flying altitude, Chris again relinquished control to his experienced copilot, who executed another perfect flight home.

As we drove to our house in Gary's vehicle, HK and I listened as Gary gave his wife a minute-by-minute description of our day's adventure. As he ended the account, he said, "He did fine flying us to Kentucky, but he ran over two buzzards coming back."

"Gary, you're joking, aren't you? I didn't run over two buzzards, did I?"

"Naw. I think they got out of the way at the last minute," Gary said with a straight face.

HK will live with memories of that special birthday experience inside his head for the rest of his life. He relives that exciting airplane adventure as if it happened yesterday. He thanks Gary frequently for his fabulous birthday surprise, and Gary always reminds him about the close call with two buzzards.

CHAPTER 22

—⁄⁄⁄—

Proud to Be a Rotarian

R otary International is a worldwide service organization that brings together business and professional leaders to provide humanitarian services, encourages high ethical standards in all vocations, and advances goodwill and peace around the world. My affiliation with Rotary has played a key role in my professional and personal life. I was a charter member of the Brentwood Rotary Club, served as its third president, and have been active in it for almost twenty-five years. Club members, mostly local business professionals, meet every Wednesday morning for an hour of breakfast, club news, and to hear a guest speaker.

During HK's summer breaks from school, he was forced to spend a lot more time in the chicken restaurant, depending on Pearl's work schedule. The summer a year after meeting HK, I got the green light from Rotary members to invite him to our weekly club meetings. It provided the perfect opportunity to get him out of the restaurant while Pearl worked.

It took him no time at all to capture the heart of every club member with his humor, wit, and infectious smile. He inspired this group so much that the board of directors made him the club's first Honorary Rotarian, a title he cherishes even today. Honorary membership entitles him to all the breakfast he can eat at weekly meetings without paying dues.

One year, not long afterward, our Rotary Club leadership decided to surprise HK with a Christmas present—the latest model exercise treadmill. They believed this machine would provide the perfect incentive for improving his muscle tone, stamina, and walking skills. He could supplement his weekly trips to Vanderbilt for physical therapy with regular year-round exercise.

Pearl agreed to the plan, so six Rotarians and I made a mid-December special delivery to her East Nashville home. I vividly remember entering the house to the homey sound of Gene Autry crooning "Rudolph the Red-Nosed Reindeer." As we unloaded and assembled the treadmill, we could not help but notice how sparsely furnished the house was. There was no table or chairs in the kitchen, or anywhere else, for that matter. The kitchen was even missing a stove. HK later explained that they often brought food home from Mrs. Winner's, or Pearl occasionally cooked a simple meal on a two-burner hot plate. Twin beds, one for each occupant, sat in a small bedroom filled with boxes stacked around the walls and reaching nearly to the ceiling. The two mattresses were the only soft items I noticed in the whole house.

Santa's Rotary Club elves kicked into overdrive and returned to Pearl's East Nashville home within days. This time even more surprises filled their sleigh. The austere kitchen was transformed with the arrival of a new table, complete with four soft-padded chairs, and the latest model four-burner range and oven with a digital integrated thermostat.

But that was not all; one last surprise awaited them. The next day while HK was at school and Pearl worked, Stu Brandt and I returned to the house and spent five hours painting the drab kitchen a sparkling shade of white. Pearl and HK pulled into the driveway just as we finished cleaning our paintbrushes. She was speechless, completely overwhelmed by the holiday shocker. HK, never speechless, complimented the two amateur painters as though he could see their magnificent artistry, saying, "Our kitchen is the most beautiful kitchen in the world! Mr. Bradford, you and Stu sure did a good job."

Our Rotary Club always scheduled many service projects around the Christmas holidays. We have a long history of cosponsoring an annual Christmas party for underprivileged children at the Tennessee Baptist Children's Home. Located on a spacious tree-lined campus near the outskirts of downtown Brentwood, this facility provides residential services for children without parents or who are unable to live with parents or other relatives.

Every December club members meet on a designated Saturday morning at a local department store to shop for gifts. We have always been able to count on the store's management to generously support our efforts by providing coffee and donuts before shopping, dedicating checkout lanes exclusively for Rotary shoppers, and, best of all, giving substantial discounts on all our purchases.

HK has an emotional connection with children, and he would not miss this annual Rotary shopping event for anything. The first year HK joined us, the project chairman designated him the shoppers' "Head Elf," a title he has continued to hold every year since. HK addressed the assembled club shoppers that day, saying, "I'm proud to be a Rotarian. Today's shopping is for a good cause, so please spend your money wisely."

The two of us shopped as a team and tried to choose gifts suitable for boys his age. HK contended that he knew exactly the best gifts for teenage boys. He insisted while shopping that I thoroughly explain each potential present in detail, including the color, style, and size. He carefully held each item before making his final selection, allowing his fingers to gently explore the item. If everything met with his approval, he finally declared, "This is a perfect gift for our boys."

Teams budget a certain dollar amount to spend for each child, and throughout the shopping trip everyone was constantly forced to recalculate their shopping cart values to stay within budget. But not us. HK, the human calculator, continually updated the amount spent and remaining funds available. It was like shopping with a live cash register. When we reached our budget amount, he would immediately say, "Mr. Bradford, that's all we can spend!"

HK wasn't bothered that we were the last team to finish our shopping assignment. He declared to anyone within hearing distance that we were the world's best shoppers. When at last we finally entered the checkout lane, he shared a closing message with our female cashier.

"I'm glad you waited for me and Mr. Bradford, because selecting the best presents requires a lot of time and patience. We are two really, really, really great shoppers."

She just winked at me and laughed.

On the following Thursday night after our shopping trip, Rotary Club members gathered at the children's home, just a few miles south of Brentwood, for the annual Christmas party. HK and I, fellow Rotarians, other financial sponsors, the children's home staff, and a few family members always looked forward to this special holiday event. It included a delicious meal, musical entertainment, and a gift exchange that filled both the recipient children and the gift givers with untold joy.

Undeniably, the children's opening of their gifts was the highlight of the party. HK introduced himself and played with many children as they opened their presents, especially the boys. He explained in great detail how he had personally selected each gift and confidently reassured every recipient that they would be pleased. Finally, he entertained the room like a seasoned performer, telling many of the guests the days of the week on which they were born.

I'll never forget what he said as I drove him back to his grandmother's house after the party: "I'm sorry some of those children don't have parents. It's sad they don't have a home to go to for Christmas. Christmas is a special time for families. I'm glad that I have Grammy and we have a nice warm house."

- ~~~

CHAPTER 23

Divine Intervention

Harpeth Hills Church is one of many in the Nashville area that actively supports a community-based outreach program called Room in the Inn. It is an annual program that begins in November and continues through March. Each night during these winter months, various churches host groups of homeless men and women, providing them a hot meal and a warm place to sleep for the night. A group of church volunteers uses the Family Life Center on Thursday evenings to provide fourteen men a hot meal, a comfortable place to sleep, a shower, laundry facilities, access to a clothes closet, and a hot breakfast the next morning.

One cold February Thursday night, I volunteered to assist with our church's Room in the Inn guests. Since HK and I have a standing Thursday Boys' Night Out, I took him along, thinking it would provide another new experience for him—one that might teach him something about the less-fortunate citizens around our city.

As we drove into the church's parking lot, I carefully explained to HK about our evening's guests. Some men were just down on their luck while others were homeless and lived on the street. I gave him a few pointers about conversing with our visitors: "You can talk with them; just don't ask them about their hardships. Share things about your life and ask them questions about things they might enjoy discussing, such as their birthdays and maybe their hometowns."

Most nights the host group has a hot meal prepared and ready to serve when the nightly guests arrive. But on this night, the Boy Scout troop responsible for cooking had gotten a late start, and the meal was far from ready. As we entered the building, fourteen homeless men were sitting together at one of several large round tables in the open gymnasium area. They were drinking coffee, patiently waiting for hot food. The strange voices were like a powerful magnet to HK's sensitive ears.

I left him sitting alone near the empty food line because I needed to ask about the evening's work assignments. I told him I'd be right back after getting my instructions. I walked away, thinking he would be content to sit and listen. I should have known better. A coworker interrupted my conversation and pointed toward HK's chair. When I spun around, he was taking his slow, short baby steps toward the men's voices. Both arms were extended for balance and rotated back and forth as he walked. He moved like a small humanoid robot.

I made a beeline toward him, but it was too late. The men had already spotted HK, and he was beginning his introduction. I reached him and gently placed my hands on his shoulders just as he said, "Hi, my name is HK. Are you the homeless people?" In unison, most of the group responded, "Yes." A couple of them even laughed at his innocent question. A well-groomed young man, probably in his midtwenties and looking somewhat out of place, said, "Hi, HK."

"What's your name?"

"I'm Anthony."

"Hi, Anthony. How did you lose your house?"

A few men laughed.

"HK, I've made some bad choices in my life."

"Anthony, I hope you get your house back someday."

In a feeble attempt to politely change the subject without offending anyone, I asked HK, "Why don't you tell these gentlemen something about yourself?" He told them about the accident, his survival and his mother's death, living with his grandmother, meeting me, and going to school. But he never mentioned anything about his father.

Then he began asking for birthdays, immediately following their answers by telling them the days of the week on which they were born. They were amazed, as people always are. But unlike HK's normal group of admirers, these guys had no way to confirm this surprising tidbit of personal trivia, short of calling family. I remember thinking, *What if an innocent encounter with my little blind friend helps these men reestablish long-lost family contacts?* You never know how God will work in the lives of desperate men.

At last the food was hot and ready. The men shuffled through the serving line, loading plates with country ham, fresh vegetables, garden salad, and piping-hot homemade rolls. I prepared HK's plate, and we joined a table with a group of our special guests.

Between bites, he continually talked and entertained everyone with his barrage of questions and funny comments. He asked about their hometowns, their ages, and how long they had been in Nashville. He even asked a few men point-blank if they had spoken with their mothers recently, emphasizing how important it was to stay in touch with one's mother. I couldn't help but notice tears streaming down the cheeks of one of the older men.

For the first time in our relationship, I witnessed the raw power of HK's message and his magnetic pull on people of all stripes, from all walks of life. That night he articulated the story of his embattled life boldly, without a hint of bitterness or despair. My precious little blind friend, with every worldly reason to be empty, angry, and miserable, instead conveyed a beautiful tale of eternal hope, unfettered redemption, and overwhelming optimism through his life story. His message was pure gold to those men without a home.

Later, as we reentered the frigid night air, I was convinced we had been summoned that night to Room in the Inn for a reason. For me it ranked as one of the best Thursday evenings I could remember, and I think that also held true for HK. I would not be surprised to someday learn that a man's life had been changed by his encounter with HK on that bitterly cold February night.

Celebrity status followed HK everywhere, even to church. A particular group of ladies searched for him each Sunday just to plant lipstick-laden kisses on his forehead and cheeks. His regular refrain, "You don't look a day over eighteen!" certainly didn't hurt his prospects for continuing female adoration. Sometimes he left church services with so much lipstick plastered on his face that I accused him of looking like Barney after Thelma Lou had worked him over. I was certain some women, who shall forever remain nameless, applied fresh lipstick just to be sure it made a lasting impression. He cherished the attention. Much to Brenda's chagrin, he preferred leaving his lipstick-smeared face untouched for as long as possible.

He loved Sunday school classes and continued making new

church friends as years passed. Interaction with his peers certainly helped develop his engaging personality. One Sunday morning as I retrieved him from Sunday school class, I overheard a young boy reciting books of the Old Testament. Later, at home, I inquired about the assignment.

"The other children were asked to memorize the books of the Old Testament," he told me.

"What about you?" I asked.

"The teacher didn't ask me to do it."

I said nothing at the time. I presumed that his teacher, who did not know the details concerning HK's disabilities, thought he would be incapable of memorizing.

While giving HK a bath the following Saturday night, I nonchalantly mentioned the Sunday school assignment. "HK, do you think you could memorize the books of the Old Testament? If you did, it would surprise your teacher and classmates. You just might do the best job of anyone in the class."

His small body immediately tensed, and he clapped his hands wildly, splattering water across the bathroom floor as he laughed. Not one to refuse a challenge, he shouted, "Yes, I want to! I know I can do it!" He prophetically added, "You know I have a good memory."

Yes, I knew he had a good memory, but at that point I had no idea as to the extent of it. I retrieved my Bible and explained how we could prepare for the daunting task ahead. Reading from the index, I slowly, distinctly, and loudly pronounced each of the thirty-nine Old Testament books, starting with Genesis. Immediately he repeated each name. We continued our process until he finished the Old Testament. Within thirty minutes he was comfortably reciting each book in order from Genesis through Malachi with only minimal assistance.

"Congratulations, HK. You're fantastic! You may have just set a Guinness World Record for memorizing the books of the Old Testament in the shortest time ever!"

"Mr. Bradford, do you think I really set a new world record?"

"Probably. Do you want to set another new record?"

"Yes. What new record?"

"Let's memorize the books of the New Testament too."

Repeating the same drill as before, we worked on naming the twenty-seven New Testament books for twenty-five minutes. He awoke early Sunday morning ready for his big reveal.

"Mr. Bradford, can I recite the books of the Bible this morning?"

"Well, I sure hope you can."

He laughed and without hesitating began with Genesis and slowly repeated every book of the Bible until he reached Revelation. The grin on his face told me he was wide awake and ready for his Sunday school surprise.

Arriving at his classroom that morning, I told the teacher, "Good morning. HK has a little surprise for you and the class today."

Clearly puzzled, she looked at HK, smiled, and said, "What's your surprise, HK?"

"I've learned the books of the Bible, and I want to recite them to you like the other kids are doing."

Caught off guard and a little skeptical, she smiled and cut her eyes my way, expressing a mixture of curiosity and doubt. Maybe she thought this was a joke.

"Class, please be quiet and listen carefully. HK will recite the books of the Old Testament."

"Miss Jan?"

"Yes, HK?"

"I don't want to recite the books of the Old Testament."

"Oh, forgive me. I thought you said you wanted to name all the Old Testament books."

"I want to recite *all* the books of the Bible."

She was clearly more confused than ever. "O-kay. . . . That sounds pretty impressive to me. Class, please listen. HK is going to recite the books of both the Old and New Testaments."

Without hesitating he began his recitation. He pronounced each name methodically and carefully in a calm speaking voice, displaying the same confidence he had exhibited while practicing. He named each of the Old Testament books and immediately plunged into the New Testament books, all the while exhibiting none of the muscular spasms usually caused by extreme excitement.

Desperately fighting tears, Miss Jan broke into spontaneous applause, joined immediately by the rest of HK's amazed young classmates. They would have been even more impressed had they known he had accomplished this feat in a mere fifty-five minutes while splashing in the bathtub!

Until then Brenda and I had no solid evidence of HK's remarkable memory. We knew he had an amazing gift for dates and was blessed with excellent recall of people, places, and events. But this episode marked the beginning of even more manifestations of his unusual abilities.

CHAPTER 24

—ᴍ—

William Returns

I t was late winter 2006, when Pearl greeted the day grumbling, just as she had done most mornings of her life, but on this day there seemed to be little apparent reason. Fifteen-year-old HK had stayed overnight at the Tennessee School for the Blind campus, as he did one night a week, and so Pearl was able to sleep later than usual that morning, taking advantage of having the house to herself.

The weather forecast called for cold rain, yet another winter storm system bringing precipitation to middle Tennessee. Pearl couldn't put a finger on it, but she had something like a premonition. Nothing in her world seemed wrong, yet some vague, unidentified uneasiness bothered her. Something bad seemed to hang in the air that day, and it wasn't just the dreary weather.

Off work and with little on her agenda that morning, she was in no hurry to get dressed, eat breakfast, or tidy up the small kitchen.

———

Midmorning the phone rang, and an unknown woman's raspy voice greeted her from the other end. She introduced herself as a friend of William's and gave her a message: "Your son wants to see you." Without hesitating Pearl blurted out, "He knows where we live, and the phone number hasn't changed." *Click*, and Pearl ended the conversation.

Her head spun for a moment after she hung up the phone. She had prepared herself to one day hear news of William's death—resolving years ago that he had most likely self-destructed and flamed out of this world with a bang—but she was not prepared for the prospect of ever laying eyes on him again. An hour later the phone rang once again, and William's familiar smoker's croak rattled from the other end. It had been ten years since she had heard his voice.

William bobbed and weaved his way through a tangle of tales describing his lost decade. He started with the last time Pearl had seen him—that day he left her at the gas station and headed for a day job in Columbia. He explained that he had had no intention of disappearing permanently, but later that night, with a little money in his pocket, he admitted getting high on alcohol and drugs. Then he hit a city police car and got locked up on multiple old and current charges. His benevolent employer and quasi-friend who had always looked out for him paid a bondsman to have him released from jail. But instead of honoring the conditions of his release, he hightailed it across the state line, met a woman in a bar, and began residency as a new Alabama citizen. He watched his back, settled down mostly with the new girlfriend, and stayed out of the law's reach for almost ten years.

Pearl told me that William never shared with her what brought him back to Tennessee, but trouble followed him home. Maybe after ten years he thought memories would fade and the police would no longer be interested in a long-forgotten fugitive from justice. Maybe on "the grass is greener" principle he thought life in Maury County would be better than in Alabama. Maybe he thought his appearance had changed enough that he could settle in there without being recognized. What he had not counted on, however, was his inherently rotten luck.

One day while he was taking a fast-food lunch break, his sister-in-law happened to be eating in the same restaurant. She was shocked when she faintly recognized her husband's long-lost brother. Keeping a low profile, she found a nearby telephone and called the Maury County sheriff's office.

Police came and gladly took William to jail on a laundry list of outstanding charges going back years. A rookie public defender got him released on probation due to his long record of good behavior. He settled into Maury County life with another girlfriend, working sporadically as a roofer during the day while delivering pizzas at night.

But soon a little extra spending money stirred up William's sleeping demons. While delivering pizzas drunk, he was arrested for DUI. This new seizure resulted in a probation violation that, in turn, caused all his previous charges to be reinstated. He promptly landed in the Maury County Jail and eventually got shipped off to state prison to serve the better part of a year.

Now he desperately needed something and had no one else to turn to, so he called Pearl. He was due to be released on parole in about thirty days, but an important condition for parole release was having a residential mailing address for at least ninety days. His only reason for calling her after ten years was to ask for a place to live while out on parole.

Pearl remembered how life had been with William in the same house, and she did not want to relive it. He was a heavy smoker, and she had found evidence of drugs when he lived there before. She wanted no part of him in the house, especially since HK had serious asthma and bronchitis flare-ups. "That's just not happening again," she told him.

Instead, she hatched a crazy idea on the spot and offered it during their conversation. She explained that she needed more storage space out back and had considered buying a storage shed, but her budget could not handle it. What if she bought the materials and he built her a shed to live in for ninety days? She figured he couldn't tear it up too badly during that short time. Then he would move along somewhere else, leaving her a practically new storage building. He gladly accepted her offer.

I never heard news of a tearful mother-son reunion on that Tuesday, March 3, 2006, and I think I'm safe in presuming it didn't happen that way. HK told me, however, that his daddy did give him a hug and said, "I'm building me a place to live." HK remembered being excited about getting to know something about his dad.

One thing William could do well was carpentry. So in a matter of days, a spiffy-looking, gray-and-white, eight-by-twelve storage shed with a single window sprang up in Pearl's backyard. William had a place to call home and a mailing address for ninety days. The only immediate problem he faced was the lack of plumbing and electricity. Pearl allowed him in the house when he needed to use the indoor plumbing, and he commandeered a long extension cord to light up the shed. This arrangement seemed to work just fine for all parties. After all, it was only temporary.

The family's adjustment to having William back in their lives took awhile, especially for HK. Not long after his father's return, I began noticing a somber change in his normally bubbly personality. He seemed withdrawn and preoccupied, and he appeared to be struggling with something. I feared he might have an undetected medical issue. But after talking more about it with him, the home-life picture became clear.

"Grammy won't let him smoke in the house, and he doesn't like it. He and Grammy scream at each other a lot."

William was getting on Pearl's nerves, and she anxiously counted the days until his next move. She had no idea where he might land, but she did not care. She just knew they would finally be rid of his explosive, unpredictable rage and its negative impact on her and HK.

Pearl's recollection of Saturday, May 20, 2006, still causes her to shudder. It was one of those rare occasions when William was on his best behavior and allowed in the house. The estranged family sat at the kitchen table, watching the televised broadcast of the Preakness Stakes, the "second jewel" of horse racing's Triple Crown. William had always complained of aches and pains from hauling shingles on his roofing job and the few other strenuous odds-and-ends jobs passed over by other day laborers. He never thought about his health and seldom visited a doctor. While watching the televised horse race, he complained more than usual of pain, especially around his chest. Pearl found an aspirin and gave him a glass of water, but the dull chest pain got progressively worse. No one knew it at the time, but William was having a heart attack. He survived and came home with two new stents holding open his clogged artery. The hospital booted him out after only a day because he had railed at, threatened, and berated the nursing staff.

It was a wake-up call for everyone but William. He throttled back his smoking habit but kept his other vices in high gear, including drinking and drugs. The most disturbing result of the crisis was that the damage to his heart changed his mind about finding alternative living arrangements. He had an old truck, zero responsibilities, and absolutely no motivation to leave his backyard nest. A modest monthly social security disability check eventually began appearing in his mailbox like clockwork. It seemed that Pearl and HK were stuck with him for good.

Pearl occasionally found him in a good mood, but at other times she complained, "He's a gigantic pain in the butt." He rarely ventured into the house unless invited, choosing instead to eat, shower, and wash clothes when they were not there. Pearl believed he had given up drinking in recent years because HK could no longer smell alcohol when he came around. William's life depended on the goodness of strangers, girlfriends, and bar buddies, and he had no sense of priorities. HK once shared that the same tire on his daddy's truck always ended up flat overnight. Rather than paying some measly amount to have it plugged, he just aired it up with an old bicycle pump whenever he needed to go somewhere.

It was a blessing that HK was well past his formative years when William came back into his life. Pearl had filled her grandson's mind with an uplifting sense of positive reinforcement, so nothing William could ever do or say could change that foundation. HK never talks much about his father, but when something does come spilling out, it certainly sounds like the father-son roles are reversed. He has said to me more than once, "My daddy has made some poor life choices, and I wish he could get his life together." I'm suspect HK has endured terrible language, bitterness, rage, and wild mood swings. I take comfort in knowing that my young friend sees clearly that this type of negative behavior adds up to nothing more than the shadow of what a man should be and that he has progressed beyond the point of having his life darkened by that shadow.

CHAPTER 25

— ᴍ —

Driving and Riding Blind

Two years after meeting HK, Brenda and I, along with close family friends, purchased equal interests in a home on Tims Ford Lake near Winchester, Tennessee. The scenic, two-hour drive from Brentwood and anticipation of glorious sun-filled days on the beautiful reservoir has always provided us a refreshing respite for our busy lives.

We wasted little time asking Pearl's permission for HK to spend summer weekends at the lake with us. Our logic, which had worked pretty well up until now, was that he could have more time with us while enjoying the healthy outdoors with sun and fresh air—a better alternative to sitting alone at the restaurant. He was thrilled with the idea and, once again, Pearl graciously approved.

It took HK little time to adjust to the lake home and its surroundings. He enjoyed his bedroom, which had a closet and a chest for medications. The house also came complete with a wide-screen television for the young sports enthusiast. We did not, however, allow him to be a couch potato. We made sure his exercise needs were not ignored. Our covered, lakeside boat dock housed a late-model pontoon boat, but getting to it required navigating fifty steep steps from the back deck down to the lake below. Everyone got plenty of exercise navigating these steps.

Brenda enjoyed as much time on the lake as possible, and it didn't take much to convince HK to join her. Hands down, his favorite lake activity was riding in our pontoon boat. Our presailing ritual consisted of removing his shirt, shoes, socks, and braces, drenching him with high SPF sunscreen, and slipping on his life vest.

The driver's seat was wide enough for two people, so one hot Saturday afternoon as we drifted along in a quiet cove, I said, "HK, would you like to sit with me and help drive the boat?"

He became so excited that his entire body tensed, and he could barely utter a sound. Regaining composure, he finally said, "Brenda, Mr. Bradford is going to let me help him drive the boat."

"Do you think that's wise?" Her voice sounded doubtful.

"It's okay. I'm a careful driver."

"HK, when did you start driving?" she asked. No one said a word because everyone knew the answer.

His boat-driving skills were amazing to watch. With little instruction, he learned quickly to position the steering wheel so that we traveled a straight path. Then, aided by my verbal commands to steer left or right, he could maintain a safe course wherever we went. His radiant smile displayed his absolute love for every minute at the boat's helm.

Each time we entered a congested area or began a parking maneuver, he graciously relinquished the steering wheel to me. Frequently he boasted to anyone who would listen that, not unlike being the world's best blind airplane pilot, he was also the world's best blind boat driver. It could be true, for all I know. There's not likely to be much competition in either of those categories.

We've been fortunate so far that the Tennessee Wildlife Resources Agency Water Patrol has not stopped us while he's behind the wheel. I'm not sure how I could explain turning over the helm of our boat to a young blind boy. I can just see the officer's reaction when I explained that he "sees" with his one good hand and not his eyes.

Brenda, on the other hand, says there's little reason to worry about the outcome of such a stop. She feels confident that with his ability to win friends and influence people, he could talk his way out of just about anything. I can only imagine how such a scene might unfold. The stern-looking water patrolman pulls alongside us and asks him for identification. Instead, HK replies, "We're enjoying a great boat ride. It sure is a nice day for it, isn't it, Officer?"

The unsmiling officer glares at him in silence.

"Have I met you before?" Silence.

"When's your birthday?" More silence.

"Officer, I love you."

At that point I can see the humorless officer's heart melting and a reluctant smile breaking through his unsympathetic features. "It's okay, young man. I'm going to let you go this time." Then he turns to me, the frowning scowl returns to his face, and I can see that I'm not going to escape so easily. But I'm happy to report that this worrisome little scene has not happened—yet.

In addition to boating with us every summer, HK regularly participated, from ages seven to nineteen, in a program called Saddle Up! This equine-based recreational therapeutic riding program designed for young people with disabilities is located on a large farm just outside of Franklin. The program's stated mission is to provide children with disabilities the opportunity to grow and mature through therapeutic education and recreational activities with horses. Participants learn responsibility and discipline while improving their agility, building self-esteem, and interacting with other riders and their parents, but most of all just having fun.

HK rode his horse one hour every week during the six-month riding season and assisted with its bathing, grooming, and feeding. This unique program takes kids with disabilities into an unfamiliar world of large animals and turns it into an outdoor classroom and weekly adventure. The horses depend on these special children for their daily care, and the children love it.

The season concluded each year with a competitive riding show. Participants showcased their newly acquired riding skills before an audience of their fellow riders, parents, and friends. No matter the disability, each rider was judged by the same performance criteria. For most of his years in the program, HK was the only blind rider in his age group, and his challenging routines were judged by the same standards as those of sighted participants.

Besides a participation ribbon given to everyone, the top three riders in each show class received either a trophy or a blue, red, or white ribbon for first, second, and third place, respectively. By the time HK aged out of the Saddle Up! program at age nineteen, he had collected multiple trophies, including the coveted sportsmanship trophy and the most improved rider award, along with numerous first-, second-, and third-place ribbons.

Today HK says that participating in Saddle Up! was one of the most rewarding challenges of his young life. He has exciting memories of his time learning to ride and being responsible for his horse. After twelve years he was happy to finish the program and allow the same opportunity for another child with disabilities.

With HK it seemed that every time one blessing ended, another one, potentially bigger and better, was waiting for him in the wings.

After his final ride at Saddle Up!, Pearl learned about a similar therapeutic riding program, without any age restrictions. Located on a
picturesque horse farm outside Springfield, thirty miles north of
Nashville, Paradise Ranch is the brainchild and lifelong passion
of Brent and Sharolyn Snyder. The Snyders, through their Paradise
Ranch charity (paradiseranch.org), provide life-changing equestrian
and recreational opportunities for people of all ages with special
needs and disabilities. During the past six years, a lifelong friendship has developed between this special couple and the blind boy
with cerebral palsy who loves horses.

CHAPTER 26

—∞—

Football Rivalries

I always imagined that little boys were born with a special DNA strand labeled "sports." HK's physical limitations, especially blindness, make athletic options difficult for him. His closest encounter will probably be using his good left hand to turn a radio dial while intently listening to the play-by-play action from a sports announcer. His dreams of a slam-dunk, a sixty-yard touchdown catch, or an out-of-the-park home run will only come in his sleep.

HK has enjoyed listening to radio sports broadcasts his entire life. We take for granted what a challenging task play-by-play announcers face when describing in precise word pictures action that is distant and invisible to their audience. Masters of the trade learn to add just the right mix of inflection, tone, and volume to transform their verbal descriptions into a visual masterpiece in the minds of listeners. For a sightless young boy listening on his beat-up boom box, those transmitted images can become his front-row seat to sporting events.

I recall one Saturday afternoon when HK became very animated while listening to a Vanderbilt football radio broadcast.

"Go Vandy! Go Vandy!" he yelled, clapping his hands just after the Commodores scored.

"How did they score?" I asked, not particularly listening to the game.

"A field goal."

"Do you know what a field goal is?"

"I'm not sure. I just know it's worth three points," he replied sheepishly, lowering his head.

His answer surprised me, and I began asking him other sports-related questions. It didn't take long to understand that he listened to games primarily for the exciting, action-packed play-by-play descriptions. His basic knowledge of the sporting event was limited to which team won or lost.

I had little doubt that he could quickly learn the basic fundamentals of football, but the task of explaining such a complex, detailed game to a blind boy was daunting. If only it was as easy as Andy Griffith's classic explanation in his hilarious monologue "What It Was, Was Football." How could a person blind since birth visualize a center, a tight end, a quarterback, or even a football? How could I describe fumbling the ball, jumping offside, punting, or making a bone-crushing tackle? But I took up the challenge and became his football teacher, explaining game rules, responsibility of each position, different types of plays, and the general on-field action.

Over time HK's heightened knowledge of sports truly amazed me and everyone around him. He became conversant with anyone about football, basketball, baseball, hockey, and NASCAR racing.

If some concept was not completely clear to him, he asked for a detailed explanation. In the beginning my explanations were met with "Oh, I didn't know that." Now his common response is "That's right. I knew that."

I was born and spent my young adult life in Alabama, where every resident was required to make a critical lifetime decision in early childhood—the Alabama Crimson Tide or the Auburn Tigers. I began listening to Auburn football games in my grandparents' rural, north Alabama kitchen when I was thirteen. It was 1957, and our beige Crosby electric radio, perched on a small metal table by the kitchen window, cracked and popped as it strained to receive the thousand-watt signal of WJMW-AM, the only radio station in the entire county. Flanagan Lumber Company, whose local owners were Auburn graduates, sponsored Auburn football radio broadcasts in my small hometown of Athens, Alabama.

HK had never been exposed to Auburn sports until we started listening to Saturday games during the 2000 football season. The inspirational Auburn fight song, combined with the constant chant of "War Eagle!" and a little encouragement from me (okay, maybe more than just a little), helped mold him into a rabid Auburn fan. Many Saturday afternoons he transformed our rec room into a full-volume Auburn Tigers cheering section, much to the delight of our subdivision neighbors. I'm certain the decibel level coming from our house enabled them to track the progress of every game from kickoff to the final gun.

Loyalty is everything when discussing football in the state of Alabama. The rivalry between the Alabama Crimson Tide and the Auburn Tigers is real, intense, and personal. Sometimes Alabama residents are forced to step back, hit Pause, and overlook their next-door neighbors hoisting an Auburn Tigers flag on game day. Occasionally, in order to maintain Christian fellowship, they pretend not to see their church friend's car plastered with the Alabama elephant mascot, complete with a personalized "Roll Tide" license plate. Family reunions in Alabama can be touch-and-go during the month of October.

I was convinced that HK's rock-solid Auburn allegiance might finally be compromised one Sunday morning at church. We were surprised to be introduced to the daughter of legendary Alabama football coach Gene Stallings and her family. As it turned out, they also attended church with us and, like most Harpeth Hills regulars, they knew about HK's life story and our journey together.

Coach Stallings guided Alabama's Crimson Tide to a national collegiate football title in 1992. His family had recently buried their forty-six-year-old son and brother, Johnny, who had lived a lifetime with Down syndrome and a congenital heart defect. HK had touched his daughter's tender heart so much that she made sure her famous dad knew every detail about him.

Once, while in Nashville on a speaking engagement, Coach Stallings extended his stay an extra day to spend time with family and, most importantly, to meet HK. His daughter had prepped us with news of her father's upcoming church visit, so we arrived a few minutes early that Sunday morning. Once everyone was settled, Coach Stallings turned around in his seat, smiled, and said, "You must be the HK that I've heard so much about."

"I am. Are you Coach Stallings?"

"Yes, and I am so proud to meet you, HK."

"Coach, I'm proud to meet you too."

Then, right on cue, HK surprised us all when he said, "Coach Stallings, you were born on Saturday morning, March 2, 1935, in Paris, Texas, and you were a big baby."

The coach laughed, his expression conveying his utter surprise. "How in the world do you know that?"

"Your daughter told me your birthday. Didn't she tell you that I have a special gift? You do know I am famous, don't you?"

Everyone around us began laughing but quieted immediately as the worship service started. The famous coach turned around several times during the worship hour to check on HK, patting his knee and smiling at Brenda and me. His face displayed a serene expression indicating, at least to me, that the little pickpocket was well on his way to adding yet another name to his growing list of victims.

Our families visited a short time after church, capturing precious photos of HK and his new buddy.

"HK, send me one of those pictures."

"You know I will. By the way, Coach Stallings?"

"Yes, HK?"

"War Eagle!"

I knew right then and there that HK had come to his senses and made a full recovery from his near–Crimson Tide conversion. The room burst with laughter as Coach Stallings, in his deepest, sternest coach's voice boomed, "Boy, what did you say?" HK laughed so hard he could barely make a sound.

Memories of meeting the celebrated football coach were imprinted on his mind forever. He remembered rubbing his fingers over the large national championship ring, and noting how heavy it felt. He expressed sorrow in Johnny's passing a few months earlier and regretted not meeting him. His new friendship blossomed each time Coach Stallings returned to Brentwood.

During one summer visit just before HK's birthday, Coach Stallings surprised him with a University of Alabama wristwatch. He considers it one of his most cherished worldly possessions. Rarely at a loss for words, HK sputtered, "Coach Stallings, this is the most beautiful watch in the whole world!"

"Well, thank you, HK. You wear it with Alabama pride."

"Coach, when Auburn plays Alabama, I'm still going to be for Auburn."

Not to be outdone by his new buddy, Coach Stallings's booming voice shot back, "Boy, how many Auburn watches do you have?"

Laughter filled the room as HK replied sheepishly, "None."

CHAPTER 27

The Game Jersey

Through his growing legion of friends, HK was afforded many opportunities to meet professional and college athletes. Without a doubt, his favorite professional football player was Kevin Mawae, a seventeen-year NFL veteran and eight-time NFL pro bowler who played center for the Tennessee Titans. HK's introduction to Kevin in 2006 began an enduring friendship that gave HK bragging rights with his school classmates until Kevin's retirement from professional football three years later.

When you consider the content of their first conversation, it's a wonder their friendship ever got off the ground. Someone had informed HK that Kevin had played college football at Louisiana State University, a dreaded rival of his beloved Auburn Tigers.

"Kevin, you know I'm an Auburn Tigers fan."

"That's okay. Auburn's not too bad."

He hovered over HK like a papa bear over his little cub. They talked, held hands, hugged, and had a picture taken together. Several times I noticed the professional football player, who stood well over six feet and weighed 295 pounds, wipe tears from his eyes.

"HK, have you ever attended a Titans game?"

"I went to a preseason game in August at Vanderbilt stadium with a group from my school, but I've never attended a regular season game at the Titans' stadium."

"Would you like to attend a game this season and sit in a skybox with my wife and family?"

As you can imagine, HK became very excited and was unable to speak for a full minute—a rarity for him.

"Yes!" he finally blurted. Then he added, "Kevin, are all of the Titans' games sold out?"

"Yes, HK, every game is a sellout."

"I don't know why the games are all sold out. The Titans are just no good!"

In his innocence HK may not have been the most tactful fan, but he was honest. At this point in the season, the Titans were mired in their division's last place with a miserable 1–5 record. Kevin winked at other nearby onlookers, shook his head, and laughed along with a roomful of people.

"HK, you're right. We stink. Maybe we'll play better if you cheer for us and attend our games."

Kevin was pretty perceptive because when HK started cheering the games regularly on TV, the Titans started winning. In fact, they won seven of their last ten games, finishing the season with a respectable 8–8 record.

Kevin saved his special skybox invitation until the week before the most important game of the season. The Tennessee Titans faced the Indianapolis Colts and their great future Hall of Fame quarter-back, Peyton Manning. HK was nearly delirious when Kevin called to invite us to the game.

Game day arrived, and we made sure to be at the stadium an hour before kickoff. Thanks again to Kevin, we were able to park in a special reserved area near the stadium entrance. HK, decked out in his Titans practice jersey and visor that Kevin had supplied, looked every bit a Titans fan that day.

We rode a special skybox elevator to the top level, high above the playing field. HK excitedly told the elevator operator, "I'm a friend of Kevin Mawae, center for the Titans, and we are going to sit in his skybox."

"You must be an important person. That's a big honor to sit in a skybox."

"My name is HK, and I'm famous. What's your name?"

"My name's Horace, but I'm not famous. It's nice to meet you, HK."

We finally reached a skybox door with Kevin's name on it and were met by his wife, their son and daughter, and a group of family friends. Located on the stadium's western 10-yard line, the spacious skybox contained a dozen comfortable theater-style seats, a restroom, a dining area, and a huge retractable window overlooking the playing field. His wife opened the window before kickoff to give us a spectacular view of the gridiron. It was like watching the game on a gigantic television screen.

From the opening kickoff, everyone except HK anxiously followed the action from the large open window. Instead, he settled into a tall chair positioned at the food bar directly behind where the others were sitting. His window on the game came from a small, handheld radio and the distinctive sound of Mike Keith, the voice of the Tennessee Titans. Large headphones allowed him to hear Mike's exciting play-by-play description approximately eight seconds after the live on-field action.

The game's two most exciting plays occurred during the final minutes. The Titans, playing their best game of the season, led the Colts from the opening kickoff. With less than two minutes remaining, the Colts drove down the field and scored on a perfect Peyton Manning pass. With the extra point, they were now tied at seventeen with a minute left in regulation play. Everyone was braced for overtime, but the Titans had other plans.

The fired-up Titans returned the ensuing kickoff to their own 30-yard line, and the offense moved the ball across midfield in three plays. With only seven seconds remaining and the score knotted at 17–17, the Titans called their final timeout before sending their field goal kicker into the game for a sixty-yard attempt into the wind. It would be a team and individual record if he made it.

The air in the stadium was electric with emotion. Every fan except one now stood, nervously awaiting the game-winning field goal attempt. With headphones muffling the crowd noise, HK leaned forward in his chair, tense with anticipation. He grimaced, as if all the pressure rested on his shoulders, while his arms extended upward as if he were protecting the kicker. He hardly breathed, intensely focused on Mike Keith's voice.

As play resumed, the kicker trotted onto the field and took his position behind the massive offensive line. The referee started play, and there was an eerie hush over the entire stadium. The kicker had never attempted a field goal this long in his entire career. The center snapped the ball perfectly, the holder caught it and placed it in the exact position, and the determined kicker approached and struck the ball solidly with his right foot. The ball shot over the outstretched arms of the Colts' defenders and, sixty yards later, rotating perfectly, sailed between the uprights and over the crossbar with length to spare. The Titans had won!

The entire sellout crowd, including everyone in our skybox, erupted in a wild, raucous celebration. Everyone, that is, except HK, who remained intently absorbed in the delayed action coming through his headphones. As our celebration began to wind down, he started rocking back and forth, screaming at the top of his lungs, "We won! We won!" Everyone in the skybox turned to watch the elated boy in super-excited mode, and our celebration revved up again.

After the game Kevin unexpectedly dropped by the skybox, where he received copious hugs and congratulations from his assembled family and friends. But HK, who was now hoarse from the post-game celebration, was his main focus of attention.

"HK, how did you like the game?"

"Kevin, I really looooved it. Did you know the Titans kicked a sixty-yard field goal and won?"

The skybox exploded in laughter, and every single person applauded his innocent inquiry. Kevin paused and grew intensely serious.

"HK, because of our great victory today, Coach Fisher gave us our game jerseys." Pausing momentarily and swallowing hard, he added, "And I want you to have mine."

The air suddenly left the room. No one moved a muscle; there was only hushed silence in the skybox. Tear-filled eyes locked on the massive football player as he placed the extra large, sweat-soaked, grass-stained football jersey on the little blind boy's lap. Visions of the memorable Coca-Cola commercial that aired during the 1980 Super Bowl, featuring "Mean Joe" Greene tossing his game jersey to a young, awestruck boy, flashed before my eyes.

For a few seconds HK's cerebral palsy prevented him from making a sound. Regaining a breath of air and surveying the jersey's details with his probing fingers, he was finally able to utter a heart-felt, "Thank you."

"HK, you are welcome."

"Kevin, I love you. You are one of my best friends."

The hulking professional football player, who had just finished an epic afternoon battle with three-hundred-pound warriors, immediately choked with emotion.

"I love you, too, HK."

CHAPTER 28

—⚭—

Dreaming Big

HK's enthusiasm for sports presented him with unique opportunities for participation that were not limited by his disabilities. One beautiful spring Saturday morning in 2007, the pint-sized celebrity opened the Williamson County Little League season by ceremonially tossing out the first pitch. With two adults standing on either side to help maintain his balance, HK summoned every ounce of strength into his good left arm and heaved a high-arching pitch in the direction of the catcher's voice. The nimble young catcher made a spectacular grab before the ball hit the ground, and a new Little League pitching star was recognized. He returned the next three seasons to throw out the first pitch, including one year when the Williamson County Little League Association presented a check for $2,000 in his honor to our church's youth group. While presenting the large donation in front of Sunday's assembly, our minister questioned the pint-sized pitcher's technique.

"HK, what kind of pitch did you throw?"

"An eighty-mile-an-hour curveball . . . one of my slower pitches."

Convinced that he had reached the pinnacle of his baseball career, my young companion next tried his hand at basketball. A visiting South Dakota college team was in town for a holiday exhibition game against the Vanderbilt Commodores. HK had been introduced to their head basketball coach when he held the same position at Nashville's Lipscomb University. This game night his coach-friend invited HK to be their team's honorary coach.

HK delivered his pregame instructions before the team hit the court. He simply said, "Maintain a positive attitude, play good defense, make your free throws, and do not lie down in the second half." He was speaking from experience: he had cautioned the Vanderbilt football team against "lying down" just a few years before when they blew a large first-half lead.

Two seasons later HK served in the same honorary capacity for the Freed-Hardeman University Lions in their basketball contest against Lipscomb University in Nashville. In the dressing room before game time, the team's head coach asked the honorary coach if he had anything to offer the team. This time HK was fully prepared.

The dressing room went silent, his body tensed, and with a voice right at the edge of breaking into his compulsive laughter, he began.

"My name is HK." Laughter broke the silence because everyone there knew him well.

"Thank you for inviting me to sit on your bench. It's an honor. Tonight you're playing a Division I team, and you're expected to lose. However, the final score really doesn't matter. The score that really counts tonight is your attitude, your hustle, and your desire to play hard—the kind of toughness that you'll be expected to maintain all season and one that I expect you to maintain tonight." He paused occasionally when his excitement, combined with his cerebral palsy, made it difficult to speak.

"If you think big, you'll be big, you'll play big, and you'll accomplish big things. Now let me tell you about me."

Again he said, "My name is HK." This time there was no laughter.

"My mother died when I was born; my father abandoned me when I was five. I am blind. I have cerebral palsy and other handicaps that keep me from playing basketball. But those things do not stop me from dreaming, and when I dream, I always dream big. And because I dream big, I've been able to do some really special things in my life. I've ridden horses and flown an airplane. I've appeared on television, served as the mayor of Nashville, and met professional football players, which is a lot of things to do for a blind boy with cerebral palsy." Occasionally he stuttered while searching for the right words.

"I want you boys to dream big this season, like I do. If you do, you can win the national championship in sports and in life. Now, go get a victory!"

Time stood still in that locker room. For a moment there was only silence. You could almost hear a roomful of heartbeats. Only a few dry eyes remained when he finished. A lone player sitting closest to his honorary coach began to clap slowly, and one by one his teammates joined in until the locker room reverberated with deafening noise.

As the room again became quiet, the honorary coach turned toward the real coach and in a loud voice said, "I did a good job, didn't I?" All of the players laughed and started clapping louder than ever while shouting, "Let's go! Let's go! Let's go!"

I wish I could report that this story had a happy ending with the smaller Division I team coming through with an epic, upset victory. It didn't happen, but that night Freed-Hardeman played their hearts out in one of the most exciting games of the season. Barely trailing by just three points with less than two minutes left in the game, they were forced to foul in an attempt to gain possession and score the winning points. Unfortunately for them, the Lipscomb team continued on a hot streak and made eight consecutive free throws, thus securing the victory.

That night I had a front-row locker-room seat to witness the powerfully stirring, inspirational words that gushed from deep within this remarkable young boy. Those basketball players might forget that hardwood contest, but I doubt they will ever forget the inspiring message delivered that night by their honorary coach.

CHAPTER 29

—✑—

Sixteenth Birthday

On HK's sixteenth birthday, in 2006, a close friend planned a surprise that nearly clogged mail service to his East Nashville house. Just two weeks before his big day, word of his great love for birthday cards began to spread among his many friends and acquaintances. The result was that by the end of his birthday week, he received more than one hundred greeting cards from people all over the world, including a family in Scotland and the Tennessee governor's office.

This started an annual quest to exceed the number of birthday cards received from the previous year. Two years later 180 cards, some containing cash gifts, started arriving three days before his July birthday and continued throughout the month. The next year cards started arriving two weeks before his birthday and continued trickling in until mid-August, eventually totaling 590 cards from twenty-eight states, Australia, Canada, and Afghanistan. Although not officially certified by a Guinness World Record, HK proudly declared that 590 cards was an all-time record for any boy's birthday. That year, at the desperate urging of the bogged-down mailman, Pearl placed a large bucket on her front porch.

Another sixteenth birthday surprise came in the form of a gracious gift from some of our dearest friends. They had gotten wind that HK's list of lifelong wishes had always included a Florida visit and ocean experience, so they graciously offered us a week at their Florida beach house. We had to tell HK we were taking a trip because it would be impossible to conceal the preparation process, but we dared not reveal our final destination. We knew that his excitement level would be pushed over the top, so with considerable difficulty we kept the journey's end a top secret. We asked Stu and Dot Brandt, along with Dot's sister, to join us.

On a sultry Saturday morning in August, our two fully loaded vehicles headed south from Brentwood on Interstate 65 toward the Florida Gulf Coast.

At regular intervals along the route, another *Groundhog Day* experience dominated travel conversation, and the nonstop repetition began wearing us down. "Brenda, where are we going? When are we returning? Oh, Brenda, please tell me. I need to know." Strained to the breaking point, Brenda finally announced, "HK, we're heading to Destin, Florida."

It's impossible to describe his excitement and facial expression upon hearing this news. First he screamed, "I'm going to have so much fun! I can't wait to get to Florida!" The news triggered the characteristic rocking motion caused by his neuromuscular disorder, and it became so forceful that it actually caused the car to swerve.

"HK, calm down before you make the car run off the road. If we have a wreck, we can't go to Florida!"

He just laughed and continued clapping his hands and loudly singing, "Yay, yay, I'm going to Florida!" Within minutes he relaxed enough to speak calmly. "Brenda, I've never been to Florida. Why didn't you tell me where we are going? I am soooo excited!"

"Mr. Bradford and I didn't want to ruin your surprise."

"This is going to be so much fun! Brenda, can I walk in the sand when we get to Florida?"

"Yes, you can walk in the sand, play in the ocean, and do lots of fun things because this is your very own special trip."

Brenda thought telling him of the Florida destination would quiet his incessant questions, but it only instigated another series of endless repetitious inquiries. During the eight-hour drive, I lost count of how many times I heard him say, "How much longer before we arrive? Where will we eat? What will we do when we get there? Can I call Grammy and tell her where I'm going?"

Three hours later we passed uneventfully through Birmingham and made our first rest stop at Peach Park in Clanton, Alabama. A water tower painted to look like a giant peach beckons interstate drivers to make Peach Park a required stop for every carload of southbound vacationers. Chilton County peaches are world famous, and Clanton, its county seat, is the peach capital of the South. Located at exit 205 just outside town, Peach Park is a peach-lover's paradise, serving everything peachy—including fried pies, cobbler, and delicious homemade ice cream. No one complained about this brief delay to our journey.

As we headed back to our cars, someone had the bright idea to buy a sack of fried pies and save them for later. Apparently HK and Stu didn't get the memo. They started raiding that bag the moment we headed south. By the time we arrived in Destin, every delicious peach pie was gone—and I didn't get a single one.

It was nearly five thirty on Saturday afternoon when we finally arrived at our beachfront destination. HK was more excited than ever. He stepped out into the warm summer air and took in a deep breath of heavy, humid, saltwater breeze. He would enjoy his first walk on the beach after the cars got unloaded.

Our female vacation planners had scheduled the first-night dinner reservations at a nice seafood restaurant that was a local favorite. HK found his first Florida meal to be an utterly new, unfamiliar, and somewhat baffling dining experience. After our party of six was seated, he explored the large round table with his left hand.

"Brenda, why do I have so many knives, forks, plates, and glasses?"

She patiently explained the purpose of each setting on the table, reassuring him that he would only need to use a single plate, fork, and glass for his entire meal. But just when she thought she had him settled, Stu chimed in and undid everything she had said.

"HK, one glass is for your wine."

Confusion returned to HK's face. "Mr. Bradford, is Stu joking with me? He knows I don't drink wine. He's just joking with me, isn't he?"

"Yes, HK, Stu is just joking with you."

We usually ordered for HK from a restaurant's children's menu, but for whatever reason, Destin area restaurants didn't offer children's menus. So throughout our entire time there, he proudly selected from the regular adult menu, choosing unfamiliar entrees, including several that we found impossible to pronounce. For a growing boy who had never eaten fresh seafood, he was in heaven.

The sugar-white sand and emerald-green ocean of Florida's panhandle attracts generations of family vacationers every year. Based on my years of astute observation, I have determined that their daily beach routines fall into two distinct categories. The first are those Energizer beach-bunny types who walk at sunrise, maintain constant "activities" throughout the day, and retire early just as the sun dips into the ocean. Then there are those who sleep late, eat more, do less than normal, and stay up past eleven every night. Our merry band of beach bums definitely fell into the latter category.

Each morning after a late breakfast, everyone changed into swimsuits and applied lots of sunscreen. The guys headed to the freshwater swimming pool while the ladies hit the white-sand beach for maximum sun time. Observing HK swim for the first time, anyone would be hardpressed to detect blindness or any other physical difficulties. His water wings provided the freedom to swim and cross the pool from side to side. He paddled vigorously with his left arm and kicked with both legs, exercise therapy that was greatly beneficial to him. Once every hour we made him leave the pool for a brief rest on his comfortable lounge chair. But within fifteen minutes he would be back in the water, kicking and paddling to his heart's delight.

Unfortunately for us, the Gulf of Mexico remained under the influence of an early weekend storm system throughout most of our vacation week. The churning water contained a slimy green slurry of seaweed and other unknown storm debris. Conditions got even worse, with whitecaps strong enough to knock over an adult. But nothing could have kept HK out of the saltwater and his first experience in the ocean. Stu and I were there to catch him every time a wave crashed over his small frame. But even that could not deter him. Each time he came up shouting, "This is fun!"—all while spewing water and seaweed from his mouth. He was knocked down and covered in mucky seaweed so many times I thought he might start growing barnacles. These repeated wave assaults kept him tugging at his sagging swimsuit, so much that Stu and I began calling him "The Plumber." He laughed, but I'm not sure he understood why.

The Wednesday weather forecast predicted an overcast sky, high humidity, and a chance of rain—typical summer Florida weather. Right away everyone decided against another day at the beach. Instead, the girls went shopping, and the boys played miniature golf.

When I was young, miniature golf was much tamer than the challenging two-par complexes of today. This facility, located about a mile from our beach house, had a jungle theme with realistic-looking lions, tigers, elephants, and palm trees strategically placed along the eighteen-hole course. HK could barely control the excitement of his first golfing experience. Decked out in a bright yellow polo shirt, khaki shorts, and a white golf hat, he looked the part of a sharp, professional golfer. Stu and I had no idea what to expect from him during our inaugural outing.

I helped align his putts and awkwardly supported him while his left hand held the putter and struck the ball. Through eighteen holes, I had one hole in one while Stu struggled with multistroke finishes on several holes. We were both amazed—and perhaps a bit chagrined—as we watched HK sink two holes in one. We agreed it had to be a simple case of beginner's luck.

Finishing his final stroke on the eighteenth hole, HK reached inside the cup to retrieve his ball, just as he had done on the previous seventeen holes. Despite wiggling his fingers all around the inside of the cup, this time he came up empty. The surprised expression on his face was priceless. His sightless world was turned upside down by something that just didn't make any sense. How could his ball have vanished? I grinned as I realized what was baffling him. I explained that the final hole was connected to an underground pipe that returned the ball to a large bucket inside the golf course office. He breathed a sigh of relief to know that the disconcerting mystery had been solved. The world was still running on stable laws of physics.

I was the designated scorekeeper that day, and after tallying everyone's strokes, I thought surely I had made an error. So I carefully totaled them a second time. Finally, I announced, "Stu, you may not like what I'm about to say." Then slowly and distinctly, I announced the final scores. Stu had accumulated 54 strokes, HK ended up with 51, and I had a highly respectable 42! (There is, after all, some advantage in being the scorekeeper.) Immediately HK starting chanting, "Yay, I beat Stu. I beat Stu!"

I couldn't help but rib Stu about his miserable finish. "Stu, how will you explain to the girls that a blind boy beat you at golf?"

"I won't tell anyone if you guys won't," was his weak reply.

"Now Stu, you know I can't keep a secret!" HK responded.

He had earned his bragging rights, and he didn't hesitate to exercise them freely. It didn't seem to bother Stu at first, but I think hearing the constant reminders throughout the remainder of our vacation severely damaged his ego.

CHAPTER 30

—m—

Speaking to Thousands

Almost eight years into my journey with HK, it was fair to say that almost everyone Brenda and I knew had heard about my remarkable young sidekick. Shortly before his birthday in 2007, I happened to cross paths with a good friend who attended a local Presbyterian church. He extended an open invitation for HK and me to address his Sunday morning adult Bible class. He asked us to share the story of our friendship, how we met, and details surrounding HK's remarkable life.

On Sunday morning, July 22, 2007, we made our first public appearance before an audience of thirty-two adults at Christ Presbyterian Church in Brentwood. We had never done anything like this before, so we kept our unrehearsed, twenty-minute talk fairly simple.

I did most of the talking while HK added his commentary along the way. We talked about the first time we met, the reasons for his disabilities, the car wreck that claimed his mother's life, being raised by his grandmother, and the lack of a male influence in his life until he met me.

It seemed that we covered most of the topics of interest, but I was concerned about the kind of response we received. I couldn't help but notice the box of tissues being passed from one tearstained face to another. I remember thinking that after that kind of reception, we wouldn't have to worry about being called to speak anywhere again.

A year and a half later, my office phone rang one morning with another unexpected speaking opportunity. One of HK's former teachers and principal at the Tennessee School for the Blind, who was currently an adjunct professor at Nashville's Trevecca Nazarene University, wanted HK to share his story with a class of future special education teachers.

Perched confidently on a tall wooden stool in front of a classroom of aspiring educators, HK shared his special education experience with the poise of a seasoned public speaker. He named specific teachers and told how they had helped him overcome his multiple limitations while encouraging him to be a better student. He named teachers, such as Phyllis Alfreda and Bill Schenk, who never once gave up on him. He emphasized patience as a key ingredient in developing self-esteem. He finished by telling this class of budding instructors the importance of just being a friend who believed in their students.

HK concluded by thoughtfully answering questions at a maturity level much greater than his seventeen years. At the end of his class presentation, the admiring audience offered gracious applause in recognition of his accomplishments and insightful perspective. Much to our surprise, a check appeared in my mailbox several weeks later, along with an invitation for a return engagement the next semester. This was the auspicious beginning of his budding career as a motivational speaker.

Franklin Road Academy, a prestigious private school in suburban Nashville, invited him to participate in Spiritual Emphasis Week. He spoke to a packed Wednesday afternoon assembly of three hundred grade-school students, parents, and teachers on the topics "Always Being the Best You Can Be" and "The Value of Friendships."

He started this solo presentation by explaining his love of sports and how excellence in sports required confidence, energy, and the desire to work hard. Then he told about his life and constant struggles, especially in school. Wrapping up, he said, "My friend, Scott Hamilton, the 1984 Winter Olympic gold medalist in figure skating, told me that the only disability any of us has is a negative attitude. I've never had a negative attitude. I've always been blind and had cerebral palsy, and there is nothing I can do about it. But that's okay because I rely on what the apostle Paul said in Philippians 4:13: 'I can do all things through Him who strengthens me' [NASB]. Therefore," he concluded, "when I eventually realized that I do have quite a few physical capabilities, I chose to concentrate on those rather than my limitations. As a result, I have flown an airplane, driven a pontoon boat, and ridden horses."

At the conclusion of his presentation, the entire assembled group of students and adults stood for a sustained thunderous ovation. I couldn't help but notice numerous adults dabbing their tear-filled eyes with tissue. His professional résumé expanded when he received a $100 gift card to his favorite restaurant for this solo appearance.

Whether by word of mouth or as a result of past media coverage, HK's incredible story of overcoming life's challenges and our unusual friendship began to spread. Soon we received another Sunday school class invitation. This time our audience numbered more than one hundred, and we sat on two wooden stools in front of the room.

Just as before, we told an unrehearsed version of our journey together and concluded with the same tear-jerking results.

News about our emotional story spread rapidly throughout Brentwood and beyond to groups desperately seeking an uplifting message. Within weeks opportunities to share our story appeared out of thin air as my telephone rang with more speaking invitations. Audiences wanted to hear more details about HK's life, experience his remarkable gift with dates, and find inspiration in his triumphant story against tremendous odds. I understood that desire; it was rooted in the same elements that drew me to HK in the first place.

But I had serious concerns. As I pondered the effect of our previous talks, I told HK, "If we're going to be motivational speakers and do it a lot, we need to make the audiences laugh rather than cry." He understood completely. We started rehearsing our talks, and he caught on quickly. In fact, he remembered our script so well that we only had to run through it once before an appearance.

We added humor by allowing him to share outrageously exaggerated stories about his tryout experiences for high school sports. (Well, perhaps they were more than merely exaggerated. To be honest, they were outright tall tales, which he finally admits to the delighted audience.) One example of these tales is his story about how wildly excited he became after the annual Tennessee-Alabama football game, when the Crimson Tide pounded the Volunteers. He overheard a disgruntled Tennessee fan say, "Our quarterback must be blind. He can't complete a pass."

"Folks, that's the greatest news I've ever heard!" HK deadpanned. "I'm blind, so if Tennessee's quarterback is blind, I think I can probably play quarterback on my high school football team!" The audience howled.

Later he grew serious and talked openly about his disabilities and how they limited playing with "normal" children his age. He told audiences how lonely it was to do nothing but listen to his radio all day. He spoke about how, for so many years, teachers lacked confidence in his learning abilities and had given up hope for him ever to acquire a normal high school education. He finished by emphasizing the importance of never giving up on anyone, especially children with disabilities.

"If I can do all these things with my disabilities, then surely you can do them since most of you are not disabled."

Occasionally the effects of the cerebral palsy acted in the typical way, causing HK's body to become so tense that HK needed to pause a few seconds before he continued speaking. The audience didn't mind one bit. It simply reinforced the day-to-day challenges that he has endured since birth.

Eventually our presentations evolved into a forty-five-minute pep talk from the tenacious little survivor. I found myself playing the straight man for his punch lines, Abbott to his Costello. We were a real comedic duo. Audience members clamored to meet him after every event, perhaps with a hidden desire to discover the weekday of their birth.

Most professional speakers I know admit to a case of the jitters before walking out to face a large, intimidating audience. But not HK; he simply says, "I'm blind and can't see the audience, so why should I get nervous?" That makes perfect sense to me.

Today we get more speaking invitations than we can handle, though we accept as many as my work schedule allows. His simple, uplifting message and amazing life story continue to touch lives with every public appearance. Audiences just seem to connect with this little live wire and be drawn to him like a magnet. We have carried our message to schools, churches, corporations, and civic organizations, with our largest audience being four thousand students and faculty members at Nashville's Lipscomb University. I suppose we can now both add "university lecturer" to our résumés.

When I think back on the incredible obstacles this amazing dynamo has overcome, I am simply awed by his accomplishments. Only a handful of years earlier he found it impossible to have a normal conversation. Now he speaks to thousands, spreading his message of hope and conquering adversity. This blessed irony is not lost on me.

—∿—

CHAPTER 31

The Flood

Spring arrived like a lamb in 2010. The big April warm-up, along with a normal three and a half inches of rain, created an explosion of color overnight. Trees transformed into translucent green wonders while wildflowers and their domesticated brethren emerged invigorated from their quiet winter's respite. When I slowed my frantic pace long enough to notice this miraculous annual event, I was reminded of why I love living in middle Tennessee, with its four distinct seasons.

Out-of-town guests arrived at our house on Friday, April 30, longtime family friends from Abilene, Texas. Since we had visitors, HK would stay home with Pearl that Saturday night. I would pick him up Sunday morning for church, and he would have lunch with all of us. The weekend weather forecast called for mostly rain, so we weren't surprised when a light mist began falling on Friday night.

Brenda was up early Saturday morning concocting a country breakfast of sufficient proportions to impress our Texas guests. To her it was simply a matter of Southern pride. By now the overnight drizzle had turned into a steady downpour. We thought little of it, thinking it was typical "April showers, May flowers" kind of weather. We ate a leisurely breakfast, enjoyed catching up on each other's families, and reminisced about our past glory days.

Ironically, my friend commented about the increasing rainstorm just seconds before a weather alert crawled across the kitchen television screen. I turned up the volume in time to hear flash flood warnings for Nashville and nearby areas of middle Tennessee. He pulled up a weather app on his smartphone showing heavy rain cells just west of Brentwood that were moving slowly in our direction. Breakfast table conversation quickly turned from family to the menacing weather.

Throughout most of the year, the Little Harpeth River gently meanders behind the houses directly in front of us. Rarely does it ever swell out of its banks—in fact, only once in the thirty-six years since we've lived here. Nevertheless, according to FEMA, our house on its corner lot was officially located within a flood plain.

Saturday noon found the streetside drainage ditch in front of our house overflowing into the street. As a precaution, I moved our vehicles to higher ground. By one o'clock our entire front yard was underwater, and the driving rain had not let up. Brenda suddenly yelled from another part of the house, "There's water coming through the walls of the rec room!" I rushed in to find a foot of rising water filling our lower-level rec room. We had just begun to manhandle furniture when we heard a nearby siren and saw firefighters wading through knee-deep water in our backyard. Peering out the back door, we could clearly see flames shooting from the next-door neighbor's house.

Within minutes the rising floodwaters submerged our central air-conditioning unit, causing a short-circuit explosion. Our electricity was gone, but fortunately we escaped with no fire. Other neighbors were not so lucky. Electrical explosions, sometimes accompanied by rolling flames, periodically pierced the steady drumbeat of rainfall throughout the neighborhood that afternoon. Firefighters extinguished the fire next door and hurried to the next residence engulfed in flames. We watched two elderly neighbors be rescued by boat, as the water in our rec room approached two feet deep. Finally, at exactly 4:47 p.m., we were all given five minutes to evacuate our house.

On that Saturday, May 1, 2010, Pearl was not scheduled for her normal Saturday shift at Mrs. Winner's. Instead, she drove HK to exercise therapy, and afterward they returned home in the torrential downpour. They had little interest in Saturday morning television until the Nashville stations interrupted their weekend programming for live news coverage of dramatic high-water rescues, fires raging out of control, and untethered structures floating down the interstate highway. Even then Pearl was not overly concerned about rising floodwater in her neighborhood.

Brenda and I and our Texas guests took refuge two blocks away at a friend's house that was unaffected by the relentless waters. Worried, I called HK at 5:15 p.m. to let him know we were safe but had to evacuate. I wanted to ease my mind about his and Pearl's safety. Pearl explained that they had no significant water problems, adding, "We've occasionally had some standing water during heavy rains, but we've never had any flooding problems even though the house sits in a designated flood plain." When I spoke with HK, I could tell that he was beside himself with anxiety and terribly distressed at hearing news about our flooded house. Before hanging up, he told me he loved me—twice.

———

The incessant rainfall continued Saturday night and early Sunday morning, alternating between sprinkles and downpours. By mid–Sunday morning the clouds parted, the sun emerged, and the furious deluge slowly began to recede. By seven o'clock Sunday night I was able to wade through knee-deep water in my backyard and look inside our house for the first time. It was not a sight I ever want to see again. Water stood nearly two feet deep in the rec room as furniture and other lifelong keepsakes floated in the muddy mess. Harpeth River Drive remained underwater and impassible, so cleanup efforts had to wait. All flights in and out of the Nashville airport were canceled, so our Texas guests remained at our friend's house with us until early Tuesday morning when the first flight departed for Dallas.

With the rain slowing, Pearl and HK left their house Sunday morning and headed toward Brentwood and her scheduled Mrs. Winner's shift. But they didn't get very far. There were only two routes to the interstate, and both were barricaded and under high water. "I won't be there today," she informed her manager after the return trip home. They closed themselves in the house and watched the sinister waters continue to rise.

On-duty staff at the U.S. Army Corps of Engineers Nashville District had no reason to think this two-day epic rainfall would present major problems for their water management office. The Corps of Engineers rely on a series of aging federal dams to balance multiple competing interests, including drinking water systems, barge traffic, power plants, and recreation, among many others. This U.S. Army command is charged with delicately equalizing these needs while protecting the public through a system designed for flood control. Experts within the water management office made critical decisions on the amount of water to release and maintain within each of the ten dams along middle Tennessee's Cumberland River. Their

1:00 p.m. Saturday, May 1, 2010, decision to open spillways at Old Hickory Dam, twenty-five miles upstream, would forever change the face of downtown Nashville and Pearl Derryberry's corner of the world.

I called to check on Pearl and HK several times Sunday, and each time she reported the water getting a little higher, even as clouds disappeared and the sun shone brightly for hours. First it was, "It's at our backyard fence." The next report was grimmer: "It's getting closer to our front steps." Pearl now knew it was just a matter of time before they, too, had to evacuate.

She contacted HK's school to see if their residential student cottages might be available for him. They were. At 9:45 p.m., with ankle-deep water licking at her truck tires, Pearl gathered William, HK, the walker he used at the school for his independence, their medicines, plus a few clothes and drove the back roads to get HK settled into a school cottage for the evening. Then she and William drove to north Nashville to stay with her friends. They could only offer enough room for two people, one in a recliner and the other on the couch.

On Monday morning her cell phone rang with an unexpected call from school. Flooding had shut down its aging water system, thus requiring students from around the state to be returned home. Pearl was forced to bring HK along to her friend's house. She broke the news to William that he would need to make other living arrangements, and then she picked up HK at school on the way to an abbreviated shift at the Hermitage Mrs. Winner's location. After she worked a few hours, they drove back to have a look at their East Nashville neighborhood.

Topping the hill on Electric Avenue, Pearl stopped suddenly and burst into tears. She could not believe her eyes. It took a full minute before she was finally able to describe the scene to her grandson. Her house of twenty-four years sat in the middle of a small lake. Water spilled over the street and barricades, blocking all traffic. Even from this distance she could see the floodwater resting a foot above the bottom of her front door. Dark with no electricity and lifeless with no people around, the neighborhood looked like a ghost town. They were both devastated.

Brenda and I were without a house only a few weeks until electricity was restored. Summer was now in full throttle, growing hotter by the day. Heating and air-conditioning contractors were slammed, and waiting lists for replacement units grew to astronomical lengths. As the water began to recede, we started ripping up mud-soaked carpet and tearing out wet drywall, paneling, and insulation in the lower-level rec room. Up and down our street, dumpsters in driveways sprouted up like weeds and soon overflowed with waterlogged furniture, carpet, wallboard, insulation, and all sorts of ruined personal belongings.

Fortunately we had flood insurance. FEMA representatives stayed in touch with us weekly. We found a capable remodeling crew who took the next five months putting our house back in good shape. Long weekends at the lake allowed us to relax and decompress while keeping us out of the way of busy workers. I would not want to relive the experience of this disastrous flood, but for my family it wasn't that bad. We considered ourselves much more fortunate than scores of others in and around Nashville.

Meanwhile, hordes of volunteers converged on the city with recovery efforts that far exceeded the historic flood's devastation. An army of volunteers from Harpeth Hills and other area churches swarmed to East Nashville and Electric Avenue. Dozens of hot, sweaty workers descended on Pearl's house from first light until nightfall, sorting through a lifetime of memories while ripping out flood-soaked walls.

The uncontrolled floodwaters caused physical damage totaling into the hundreds of millions of dollars, and to the thousands of people affected, they inflicted emotional suffering beyond measure. With her house filled with a foot of water, Pearl was a victim on both counts. The struggling life she endured caring for her special needs grandson collided with the flood's aftermath and propelled her into an emotional abyss. She simply could not process the abrupt and devastating personal loss. Although Pearl did have flood insurance, she was stuck emotionally in a neutral gear and found it impossible to make decisions or delve into the complex process necessary to get the recovery ball rolling. She told me, "I'm a cluttered person, and a lot of my stuff got thrown away." My guess is that she was probably on the verge of a nervous breakdown.

Fortunately our friend Gary Waller came along and offered just the right help at the perfect time. He sat Pearl down and firmly told her straight up, "You have been presented with a golden opportunity. You can rebuild this place, Pearl, in any way you want—and I will help you get it done." Gary's words and no-nonsense demeanor helped to get her moving forward again.

He contacted FEMA officials and persuaded them to hasten payments by cutting through red tape. Qualified construction crews were scarce throughout Nashville, but Gary located one and began supervising the six-month rebuilding process. Substantial improvements to Pearl's aging house included larger closets, a laundry room, a kitchen easily accessible to HK, and a ramp at the front of the house and out back. She also had the house raised onto a new foundation that was three feet higher. Both occupants would sleep much better now.

By this time I had known HK for almost eleven years. In so many ways our friend and buddy relationship had evolved into something more like that of a father and son. Memories of Nashville's 2010 flood will always stick with me, not only for its physical impact on my slice of Harpeth River Drive but also for the emotional toll I endured on HK's behalf. I have never felt more helpless than when he and Pearl needed me and the floodwaters kept me away. Gratefully our families escaped without loss of life. In a backhanded sort of way, I guess you could say that the aftermath of the flood actually did us a favor. Weekends staying out of our respective construction zones provided us with even more time with HK at the lake. This episode undoubtedly solidified my heartfelt, emotional connection with this special young boy. I loved him like a son.

CHAPTER 32

A Gift of Memory

In 2010, after years of observing HK's extraordinary ability to vividly recall dates and events, the mystery of his memory was unlocked by the same Vanderbilt medical professionals responsible for his survival miracle. He had been a patient of Dr. Tom Davis, MD, a Vanderbilt professor of neurology with a specialty in movement disorders, since his early teenage years due to his spasticity from cerebral palsy. Dr. Davis had always been fascinated by his young patient's ability to remember his medical history. He never needed reference notes of previous visits. HK could recite his medical history, including blood pressure, pulse rate, and other exam details, along with the temperature and weather conditions on the day of each visit. At the time Dr. Davis thought of these recitations as merely cute and interesting.

One day while in the hospital clinic with Dr. Brandon Ally, a

Vanderbilt memory researcher and assistant professor of neurology, psychiatry, and psychology, Dr. Davis decided to share the story of HK and his remarkable memory. "I have a patient I think you might really be interested in meeting. It seems that he can remember everything. He simply does not forget any detail that enters his brain."

The wiry, bespectacled memory specialist had just arrived at the medical school earlier that year. Along the way he had received postgraduate training at Harvard's Geriatric Psychology Lab and completed a three-year research fellowship in cognitive neuroscience at Boston University. Married with three small children, he was well prepared and ready for a medical researcher's life at the world-renowned Vanderbilt medical complex.

Dr. Ally focused his professional career on the human memory and discovering causes for why it breaks down with age and disease. With funding from the National Institutes of Health, he and his assistant used the vast array of Vanderbilt's substantial resources to conduct neuroscience studies focused on the brain. Medical science has confirmed that human memory peaks at age twenty-two. Dr. Ally wanted to understand how and why after that age the memory slopes gradually downward in some while free-falling in others.

Upon hearing Dr. Davis's revelation about his young patient, Dr. Ally was highly skeptical. One of a researcher's greatest attributes is a healthy dose of skepticism. It's a key tenet of the scientific profession and central to the quality control of research. Dr. Ally knew that everyone had anecdotes about his or her own memory. It was either great or awful, usually depending on one's age. He had lost count of the number of people who claimed to have a near-perfect memory. Only after hearing stories similar to those relayed by Dr. Davis from HK's longtime pediatric neurologist did Dr. Ally realize that there might be something to those phenomenal accounts.

Later, during one of HK's follow-up visits, Dr. Davis asked Pearl if she would be interested in discussing his memory with Dr. Ally. She said yes, and HK was beyond excited. He could finally showcase his attention-grabbing talent to a qualified memory expert who might help unlock the mystery inside his head.

Dr. Ally didn't remember the date of their first meeting, but HK did. It was Friday, January 28, 2011. Right away he performed his entertaining birthday trick, but the memory researcher was not impressed. "Everybody thinks the calendar-date thing is the coolest," he explained, "but it is not memory-related at all. It's more of a computational, mathematical process that his mind performs in seconds."

He explained to Pearl that this savant-like ability usually accompanied either Asperger's syndrome or elevated autism. HK's superior ability to recall minute details from years before was in neither of these categories. And this, Dr. Ally knew, made HK an exceptional subject for his memory research project.

Throughout the memory-testing sessions, Pearl learned that much of what is known about the brain today came from exceptional cases like that of Phineas Gage, a railroad worker from the 1850s who survived a metal rod through the brain. Resulting changes in his personality gave doctors the idea that different areas of the brain had very distinct functions.

The most-cited case in medical literature arose in the 1950s in the case of Henry (H. M.) Molaison. Doctors removed entire portions of H. M.'s brain, the hippocampus and amygdala, in an attempt to prevent severe epileptic seizures. The seizures stopped, but he lost the ability to create new memories. His surgery confirmed that these two areas of the brain were vitally important memory structures.

Though no one paid much attention to it, HK's memory had been on display from an early age. He could remember every detail of his medical history as recorded on each doctor's visit from age five. Despite his blindness, he knew his exact location at any point along the twenty-mile drive from Pearl's house to his school. He loved to remember things, whether significant or trivial. He recalled winning second place in the sixty-meter dash during the Junior Special Olympics on October 13, 1999, along with the fact that the temperature was seventy degrees that day. He vividly replayed the time he ate spinach Alfredo before watching *Star Search* on March 19, 2003.

He could remember every waking moment since around age three. Stockpiling the minutiae of everyday life, his heightened sensory receptors cataloged details from television, radio, and conversations—even those dreadful life events that most people would just as soon forget. As he explained, "I remember the negative things, but I don't dwell on them because they are just history. I think about all the good stuff."

Multiple visits with Dr. Ally and his lab manager helped confirm their diagnosis of HK's hyperthymesia, or highly superior auto-biographical memory (HSAM). The doctor explained two types of long-term memory. The first type, semantic memory, is a structured record of facts, meanings, concepts, and knowledge about the external world that we have acquired from sources other than firsthand experience. An example would be things learned from a textbook that become part of our general encyclopedia of what we know to be true.

The second type is episodic memory, which refers to our ability to reconstruct images of experiences and specific events (episodes) that took place at any given point in our lives. Remembering intricate, specific details from your wedding day, memorizing a piece of music or a poem, or recalling exactly where you were and what you were doing when you learned that the second airplane had crashed into the World Trade Center would be examples of episodic memory. All normal people experience such incidents of episodic memory, especially in relation to extremely happy or traumatic occurrences that impress our minds profoundly. But highly superior autobiographical memory goes much deeper than this.

Part of the definition, and a distinguishing factor of HSAM, is the ability to perform some sort of mental time travel, in which the mind effortlessly goes back in time to relive the distant episode just as it happened. If this element is absent, the experience remains as just an incident of ordinary episodic memory.

As Dr. Ally explained it, "If I gave him a list of ten words to remember and asked him about them twenty minutes from now (episodic memory), or if I asked him who was the twentieth president of the United States (semantic memory), HK's memory for this type of information would be little different than ours because it's more about memorizing than remembering. But if I asked what he had for dinner or what he watched on television on a specific day two years ago, he could remember it exactly. That's autobiographical memory." HK says going back in his memory is natural, it just happens. He is transported back to the scene, reliving the memory exactly as the incident happened originally, as if a videotape of it were replaying in his mind.

Because of his superior autobiographical memory, life is never dull when you are around HK. It's like always having a live Google search engine next to you.

"Monday will be the ninth anniversary of the tornado that struck downtown Nashville, Wednesday will be the third anniversary of the death of President Ronald Reagan, Thursday will be the sixth anniversary of the first time I spent the night at your house, and Sunday will be the thirty-ninth anniversary of the day man first landed on the moon."

One personal benefit of his memory is that he continually

reminds me about anniversaries of memorable events. Thanks to HK, I'm one man who will never get in trouble because I forgot my wife's birthday or our wedding anniversary. On the other hand, there are many opportunities for unintended comments to come back and cause extreme embarrassment when your best friend remembers everything.

HK and I were listening once to a Vanderbilt football radio broadcast when the Commodores were losing 37–0. Unfortunately for me, I innocently commented that college coaches are paid lots of money to win and often get fired if they lose too many games. I concluded my thought, saying, "And that just might happen to the Vanderbilt coach." HK replied, "That's so sad about coaches getting fired for not winning a lot of games."

Fast-forward two years when I had the opportunity to meet Kevin Stallings, Vanderbilt's head basketball coach. Upon hearing about my young companion and huge Vanderbilt fan, he invited us to a workout session at Memorial Gym. Coach Stallings spied us as we entered the practice facility and motioned toward seats just off courtside. Then he came over to greet us.

"Hi, HK."

"Hi. What's your name?"

"I'm Kevin Stallings."

"What's your job?"

"I'm the head basketball coach at Vanderbilt."

"Kevin, Kevin, let me tell you what Mr. Bradford said. He said if you don't win many games this year, you're going to get fired."

I stared a hole in the floor, wishing I could crawl into it while the coach assured HK that at the moment his job was on a solid foundation. Coach Stallings remains firmly at the helm of Vanderbilt's basketball program while I've not been invited back to Memorial Gym since then.

————

Dr. Ally's study showed that HK's extraordinary memory is not related to intelligence. While research confirmed his HSAM, it also showed that he had a normal IQ of 97. It was his accuracy of recollection that was off the charts. When I met HK as a nine-year-old, he had an extraordinary gift of memory—but no one knew about it. His superior memory had not yet developed to the point of attracting attention. After exercising his newfound gift for a few years, tests revealed his recollection ability at age eleven had risen to 90 percent. Today it is nearly perfect.

Using the latest structural MRI technology available at that time, Dr. Ally and his associates discovered two major factors that could help explain HK's HSAM: an amygdala four times larger than normal, with connections to the hippocampus that were ten times greater than normal. They concluded that his exceptionally large amygdala was charging every personal experience with self-relevance and emotion, turning ordinary, everyday occurrences into seminal life events. You can see from the descriptions of HK's emotional responses in this book that this diagnosis fits observed reality exactly. Every incident is elevated to the level of a grand experience.

Dr. Ally's research study on HK was published in the journal *Neurocase* in April 2012, the same journal that published the first known case of hyperthymesia in a woman named Jill Price in 2006. After the condition was named, a handful of people who possessed it were identified, including *Taxi* actress Marilu Henner. HK was only the second case to be presented in scientific literature and the first to include structural imaging data from brain examinations.

Dr. Ally and his team believe that what they learned from HK's case has the potential to change the way scientists think about autobiographical memory. A hallmark of this type of memory is imagery that the brain processes through the visual domain. HK's imaging studies indicated that regions of his brain ordinarily involved in vision were working and well connected to other brain regions despite his blindness.

In other words, the parts of the brain assigned to vision remained healthy and active, even in the absence of functioning optical apparatus. With no vision to occupy them, these parts may have turned their attention to other brain functions, such as memory, thus providing superior memory enhancement. Dr. Ally hopes one day to conduct a functional imaging study on other individuals who have been blind since birth to learn what role this region of the brain actually plays in memory.

Dr. Ally's continuing research has important implications for Alzheimer's disease. One of the first things to disappear in Alzheimer's patients is autobiographical memory, and HK's case could point to potential brain targets for deep brain stimulation or breakthrough drug therapies.

Dr. Brandon Ally moved his family to Nashville with no inkling that someone with perfect autobiographical memory lived just seven miles from the Vanderbilt campus. With wonder in his voice, he commented on this happy coincidence, saying, "Given that only a handful of people in the world have hyperthymesia, this was most definitely a once-in-a-career opportunity."

CHAPTER 33

King of the Prom

As HK began his middle school years, he struggled mightily. His autobiographical memory did not give him advantage with more advanced subjects, and he found it difficult to maintain the normal achievement level required by the State of Tennessee in order to graduate. Beginning with the 2006–2007 school year, he entered the seventh grade, studying the same curriculum as every other seventh grader statewide. After only a month he was floundering, frustrating teachers, and slowing the learning pace of his classmates. This time teachers had no choice; he was moved back one grade.

But Bill Schenk and a small handful of educators never stopped believing in HK's ability to learn. They spent the extra effort required to encourage him while he buckled down and wrestled through hard subjects every day, fully aware of what was at stake. Studying became top priority during his time at our house. Occasionally he played a radio in the background, but it never seemed to distract him. I offered as much assistance as possible, but my help was limited to little more than placing the correct textbook on his desk or loading paper into his braille machine. He knew exactly where his homework assignments began and rarely needed anything more than my eyes and hands.

HK realized the danger of being moved back a grade. It jeopardized his only chance of completing high school like a normal kid. He pushed his study time into overdrive, hitting the books for up to six solid hours each weekend, only breaking long enough for me to load paper or deliver a glass of chocolate milk. He was stubbornly persistent, determined, and obsessed with tackling his work in a way that would compensate for his academic shortcomings. He never gave up and worked only harder to prove the doubters wrong.

By the end of that school year, HK had surpassed even his own expectations. His indomitable efforts resulted in achieving honor roll status, but the best news came on the school's final day: he was told that he had met all qualifications not only for seventh grade but also for eighth grade as well. This same steady progress continued throughout his high school career. When he officially became a senior in 2011, he was academically ranked near the middle of his class.

The positive results of HK's hard work boosted his self-confidence. He took pride in his schoolwork and was thrilled when his efforts resulted in high marks. As a high school senior, his most difficult, most frustrating, and least enjoyable subject was algebra. I identified fully with that feeling. Ever since I had escaped my own high school algebra class, I had studiously avoided ever touching an $x = y$ equation again, so I was no help whatsoever. But I marveled at his remarkable ability to solve complex algebra problems using his braille computer and transferring the final answer to a braille writer.

He was not content merely to get through high school academically; he was also determined to participate in extracurricular activities. He had always dreamed of playing team sports but was realistic enough to know that it would never happen. So he compensated by becoming a wrestling team cheerleader. He also loved to sing, so he joined the school chorus.

For several years HK participated in the annual Braille Challenge competition against blind high school students from neighboring states. Nashville Mayor Karl Dean appointed him to the Mayor's Advisory Committee for People with Disabilities. As a result, HK participated in Vanderbilt University's 2012 Youth Leadership Forum for People with Disabilities and attended the National Federation for Blind Students State Convention in Chattanooga. Speaking on the Rotary Club circuit resulted in his being named an honorary citizen of my hometown of Athens, Alabama, and receiving honorary membership in five Rotary Clubs across three different states.

High school class rings were ordered during the junior year and arrived near the end of that term. This meant that incoming seniors were able to wear their rings for more than a year before graduation. HK treasured his class ring. It constantly reminded him of the enormous achievement that many had felt would be out of his reach.

I was the first person he called the day his ring arrived. The next night I picked him up for our standing Thursday Boys' Night Out. As I entered Pearl's living room, he could barely contain his excitement. He shoved his left hand high above his head to show me the shiny silver class ring set with a bright ruby-colored stone. I held his hand, admiring the ring, and realized that he was wearing it on his index finger. At first I thought the reason might be to keep it from slipping off his smaller ring finger and losing it. But I had to ask.

Wiggling his empty ring finger, he explained, "Mr. Bradford, I'm saving this finger so that when I find a girl who loves me and will marry me, I'll use it to wear my wedding ring." I just stared at him in wonder, thinking, *Is there no end to this kid's ambition?*

Midway through HK's final school year, his entire graduating class of seventeen embarked on a senior trip of a lifetime. He remembers the date as Friday, December 9, 2011. This group of blind and visually impaired students flew from Nashville to Denver, Colorado. For many, it was their first commercial airline flight. From the airport they took a two-hour bus ride to Aspen and the Snowmass Village ski resort complex. Over the next five days, these high school seniors—some, like HK, with multiple disabilities—enjoyed an unforgettable downhill alpine skiing adventure.

Specially trained instructors skillfully assessed each individual and selected adaptive ski gear to match each one's unique capabilities. By the end of the first day, each student, carefully tethered to a ski instructor, was able to feel the wind in his or her face and the hair-raising exhilaration of downhill skiing. Recalling his experience, HK proudly reported that never once during his entire time on the slopes did he ever take a tumble. In fact, the ski instructor cadre awarded him the title "Best Blind Skier Ever," and he had the certificate to prove it.

A few weeks after returning home, an envelope addressed to "Mr. HK Derryberry" arrived in Nashville. A letter, signed by every ski instructor, described how much they enjoyed getting to know him while assisting him on the slopes. They were extremely impressed by his constant cheerful attitude and concluded the letter by saying, "You touched us like we've never been touched before." A $100 Walmart gift card was tucked inside. I'm sure this was a huge sacrifice for a group of college kids moonlighting as instructors during ski season. The little pickpocket left a trail of victims wherever he went.

As if graduating from high school were not enough, HK spoke enthusiastically about the potential for attending college. The first time he mentioned this in front of Brenda, she said, "HK, that's wonderful, but you'll need someone to assist you while on campus." She looked straight at me as if to say, "And I know just who that someone will be." Then, after a dramatic pause, she began to count: "Seventy-two, seventy-three, seventy-four, and seventy-five."

"What do those numbers mean?" HK asked.

"Those are the ages Mr. Bradford will be during each of your college years. He'll probably be the world's oldest college freshman."

HK's senior prom stood out as one of his high school highlights. That night was an especially glamorous affair for the senior class, and HK did not disappoint. He impressed the entire assembly, arriving handsomely dressed in a black tuxedo and tie with a burgundy cummerbund. But his entrance caused the biggest stir when he arrived with Miss Brooke Sage on his arm, a beautiful, sighted blonde senior from Franklin High School. She was a sweet girl, one of his special friends who had asked if she could be his prom date.

HK's monumental struggles and his resilient, positive attitude in overcoming learning difficulties had inspired the entire student body. During a short intermission in prom festivities, administrators made a surprise announcement. With all votes counted, his classmates had elected him King of the Prom, one of the school's most prestigious honors.

On June 1, 2012, William HK Derryberry crossed the auditorium stage to receive his high school diploma, an achievement that had eluded both his parents. He had secured a promise from Nashville's Mayor Dean to attend the momentous graduation ceremony. The mayor fulfilled his promise and was seated on the front row with a sizable entourage that included Grammy and friends of all ages who had come to witness this special occasion.

HK's distinguished high school career was noteworthy for multiple awards and personal recognition. The mayor presented him

Nashville's Trey Pointer Young Citizen Award. That year he received the Tennessee School for the Blind's Person of Character honor.

Many years before, when my daughters arrived at the same milestone, I truly felt that time had vanished much too quickly. That same feeling swept over me as I watched HK cross the stage. I wondered what had become of that small, shy, lonely boy I first met in Mrs. Winner's restaurant almost thirteen years earlier. He was now twenty-one years old, stood only four feet eleven, weighed 143 pounds, and still looked extremely young for his age.

During those thirteen years, I witnessed his transformation from a small, isolated child who could barely talk into a confident young man full of personality, charm, and energy. He had a ready response when I asked about his future hopes and dreams.

"In addition to being a motivational speaker, I want to work in Vanderbilt's neonatal clinic after college." Then he thoughtfully explained, aware of his obvious limitations: "I'll answer the phones, talk to the parents, rock the sick babies, and tell them their lives will eventually be better, just as mine was."

And then it hit me. Although his disabilities would always be on full display, his calling card now included a large measure of charisma. It was a hidden trait that carried vast potential his grandmother never thought possible—but God knew all along.

CHAPTER 34

"I Think She Would
Have Loved Me"

Today is Friday, October 16, 2015. I'm sitting in our kitchen, sipping coffee from my Auburn Tigers mug and gazing out over the dazzling glory of autumn as it unfolds in middle Tennessee. Although the sun has shone brilliantly throughout the day, an early-morning cold front caused the temperature to slip steadily. Leaves dance in the crisp breeze before spreading themselves across the lawn, masking the final green vestige of fading summer. Tonight could bring our first frost, followed closely by a sudden reemergence of sweaters and long sleeves. I smile as memories fill my head, sweeping me back to a day a lot like this one, a day exactly sixteen years ago. It was the day I first laid eyes on HK Derryberry.

I have often wondered about my choice that day to turn left

instead of right. Looking back now, that insignificant decision had life-changing consequences. All I know is that on that particular Saturday morning, God was my GPS, and He had me on a mission.

I find it unfathomable that time has passed so quickly. My memory bank is full of a lifetime of heartwarming, humorous, and even a few embarrassing stories that characterize my involvement in HK's life. I could just as easily have missed the magnificent transformation of that small, shy boy with leg braces sitting alone in his own world at Mrs. Winner's Chicken & Biscuits.

HK celebrated his twenty-fifth birthday in July 2015, a milestone even Vanderbilt's NICU experts might consider miraculous after his touch-and-go ninety-six days in their care. I thank God every day for his maternal grandmother's decision to let him live, and I shudder when I reflect on how she could have just as easily decided against it.

Just as he tells all the ladies he meets, HK doesn't look a day over eighteen. Today he bears little resemblance to the tiny, cute boy I met on that cold autumn morning in 1999. He's taller now, his hair is neatly trimmed, and he radiates a perfect smile, thanks to braces and expert dental care, compliments of a local dentist friend and his staff. An updated, stylish wardrobe keeps him looking preppy while his engaging personality and superb communication skills attract people like magnets.

In the same way, the reflection in my mirror bears little resemblance to the man HK met sixteen years ago. I was fifty-six then, but I'll soon turn seventy-three. I'm seriously considering retirement soon. My once-brown hair is now thinning and gray; my unavoidable crow's-feet have spread. It really makes my day to hear so-called *friends* remark that I look like my late grandfather.

Brenda continues her sales rep business and is a wonderful grandmother to Mac and Catherine in North Carolina. She's involved in the lives of both our daughters and has become an expert at texting, just to stay in touch. She loves spending sunny summer days at the lake house and with friends in Florida. Friday nights are still reserved for "adult functions." We reserve this night because I'm not convinced that she enjoys all of the silly stuff that HK and I do, like singing at the top of our lungs or splashing around playing bathtub basketball. But she's gracious about it and usually doesn't say much. If the rec room noise gets too loud, she'll just close the door and go on about her business.

—⁂—

Pearl knows that life's lemons don't always translate into lemonade. She has endured more than her share of lemons in her lifetime, but she discovered a fresh crop of them on Friday, July 18, 2008, when a new Mrs. Winner's manager took over. Whether it was corporate policy or not, this new boss wasted little time informing her that HK could no longer stay in the restaurant dining area while she worked the front counter. I'll always remember her desperate phone call and the sound of her quivering voice as she asked me to come immediately and get HK. She had fifteen minutes to get him out of the restaurant, or she would be forced to leave work and forfeit a day's pay, and she couldn't afford that.

When I entered the familiar restaurant, Pearl was in tears, and HK was confused. He did not understand why he had to leave. Pearl could not quit because she needed her part-time hours. So, unhappy as she was, she reluctantly continued working under the new management. But for HK and me, this would be our final visit to Mrs. Winner's dining room.

A new Brentwood chicken restaurant, about a mile down the road from Mrs. Winner's, presented us with a fresh dining opportunity.

One trip to the Atlanta-based Chick-fil-A chain, home of "the original chicken sandwich," was all it took for us to make it our new favorite hangout. From that day on, Thursday's Boys' Night Out found us there satisfying our chicken cravings before joining friends for our usual bluegrass fix.

The fast-food restaurant's general manager introduced himself one Thursday night and instantly became HK's buddy. He loved introducing him to customers and even to occasional visiting Chick-fil-A executives. His brother, the store's owner/operator, also became enamored with HK, and together they named him the "unofficial" Brentwood Chick-fil-A ambassador.

In addition to Thursday nights, HK was now spending most weekends with us, so we added Saturday mornings to our weekly Chick-fil-A rotation. We once celebrated his birthday with the entire restaurant crew. That year they surprised him with fifty-two gift cards, redeemable for a #1 combo—chicken sandwich, waffle fries, and a drink—every week for a year. That started a birthday gift tradition that these two generous men continue to this day. I keep his valuable gift cards in my vehicle's glove box under lock and key, and hand him one each Thursday night before we enter the restaurant.

Thanks to the owner's connections with Chick-fil-A's home office, HK and I were featured devotional speakers at the company's Atlanta corporate headquarters on October 13, 2014. We made many new Georgia friends and received a thunderous reception from more than four hundred company employees. Later that day we received a behind-the-scenes tour, including a peek into the untouched office of Mr. S. Truett Cathy, the late founder, CEO, and president of the company. HK now counts the founder's son and current chairman and CEO, Dan T. Cathy, among his growing legion of friends.

I find the contrast between HK's speaking abilities when I first met him and now to be simply remarkable. At first he could not engage in a normal conversation, but now he comfortably joins me in speaking to large audiences, commanding attention and capturing hearts with his inspiring story. We've spoken one hundred times during the past five years to more than twelve thousand people and have never advertised our services. Each invitation comes strictly from word of mouth or from the website we established about two years ago (hkderryberry.com).

HK loves entertaining audiences, so we try to accept as many speaking invitations as possible. A professional speaker friend of mine once asked me about our fee structure. I remember thinking, *What fee structure?* Having seen our forty-five-minute presentation, he quickly convinced me there was a rewarding market for our talks, so we followed his advice and established one.

I am always astonished each time we receive a speaking invitation. Who would have ever thought that we would be paid to speak to audiences throughout the country? We have been keynote speakers for Goodwill Industries; treatment provider councils of Tennessee, North Carolina, South Carolina, and Georgia; and United Cerebral Palsy's 2014 annual conference in Nashville. In addition, we have spoken to many Rotary Clubs all over the South, local nonprofit organizations, corporations, schools, universities, and churches.

I've witnessed firsthand this struggling boy with disabilities living his life as close to normal as possible. HK has never been depressed or seemed discouraged in my presence, and I've only seen him cry twice—once when I told him good-bye at the restaurant, and the other after that painful hamstring surgery. When asked about his day, the standard response is always a heartfelt and booming "Lovely, lovely, lovely!"

Pearl officially retired when the chicken restaurant closed on August 4, 2013. Through prudent planning and careful spending, she and HK live a comfortable though meager life. No doubt his growing agenda will keep her young for many more years. Even so, HK realizes the mortality of human life and has some concerns about his future. He recently told me, "Mr. Bradford, if something happens to my Grammy, I have selected *you* to take care of me."

Apparently HK was not thinking about the fact that his Grammy and I are close to the same age and, in the normal process of life, it's likely that we will both be gone before he is. That is why speaking fees and other income based on HK's story, including proceeds from this book, have allowed me to establish a trust for his earnings to cover a lifetime of future care when Pearl and I are no longer in his life.

One Saturday morning a few years ago, while parked in a handicap spot in front of the local Kroger store, I sifted through my SUV's jumbled glove box searching for my hanging handicap placard.

"Mr. Bradford, what are you doing?"

"I'm trying to find my handicap placard."

"I didn't know you were handicapped!"

"I'm not, knucklehead; you are."

"Oh yeah, I forgot."

Sometimes he thinks he's the normal one.

———

One specific afternoon side trip will remain with me for the rest of my days. I was driving to Huntsville, Alabama, to visit my hospitalized brother who was recovering from surgery. Pearl had agreed for HK to tag along with me that day for the short road trip. About thirty miles south of Brentwood on Interstate 65, I noticed a sign informing me that the Columbia exit was one mile ahead. On the spur of the moment, I asked HK if he would like to visit his mother's gravesite, and he said yes.

We took the exit and turned left at the bottom of a long incline. I drove under the interstate bridge and immediately spotted the cemetery driveway on the left-hand side of the road. Turning in slowly, we passed a marble marker bearing the name of Jones Cemetery. I could not help but notice that this eternal resting place was wedged between a twenty-four-hour truck stop on one side and the interstate right-of-way on the other. The constant roar of eighteen-wheelers and incessant interstate traffic noise kept this burial ground anything but peaceful.

We were alone as I slowly drove along the gravel lane, carefully reading names engraved on the granite headstones. Peering into the bright afternoon sunlight, just to the right of the driveway, I spied the name of Mary K. Moon Davidson. I helped HK out of the car and held his hand as we walked toward the gravesite. When we reached the headstone, three things instantly caught my attention. There was a small, oval-shaped, color photograph of his mother permanently attached to the stone. The grass had been recently cut, and clippings covered the slab's bottom ledge. A small vase containing a single faded-yellow artificial flower, now nearly white, was buried in the red dirt. It had been awhile since the last visitor.

I placed HK's small left hand on the corner of the stone for balance. In a soft voice I described his mother's shoulder-length auburn hair, her dark eyes, flawless complexion, and a demure smile that perfectly matched her simple tan-and-white blouse. Tears filled my eyes as I stared, fascinated by the photo. After a short pause to compose myself, I pronounced him a spitting image of his mother. But my tears erupted full force when he sweetly said, "I wish my mother hadn't died. I think she would have loved me."

I know Mary would have loved her son, but I can't fathom anyone loving him more than I do. A day never passes that I don't think about him or mention him in conversation. He will always affirm my belief that God is still in the miracle business. I frequently consider how much better our world would be if everyone could see life the way HK does—through his heart rather than his eyes.

—⚇—

New Life Awakening

On an unseasonably cold, windy October morning sixteen years ago, a middle-aged man and a young, blind boy with disabilities, sitting at a window table in a fast-food chicken restaurant, began a life journey together. The man thought he had it all and lacked for nothing, but meeting this angelic-faced child with a sheepish grin, ill-fitting clothes, and braces on both legs shook him to his core. The young boy needed two good eyes, so he borrowed his friend's. The crippled youngster needed two good legs, so the man carried him into worlds he never knew existed. Together they explored uncharted territory, and along the way were both awakened to see the world more clearly than either of them had ever imagined possible.

The man swapped his vision of a perfect life for a nobler one. The boy opened his eyes to a new world where everyone is your friend and you are on a first-name basis with waitresses, professional football players, newspaper reporters, and country music stars. The man discovered a new reality where the air is eternally charged with fresh innocence and filled with positive attitude, a brand-new world where God-given talents delicately touch every heart. Finally, he uncovered a realm of self-proclaimed fame, where women don't look a day over eighteen and *good-bye* is no longer in your vocabulary.

Their transformations were profound and pervasive, yet both received an even greater gift—the young boy without a father found one. The man without a son did too.

—ᴍ—

Acknowledgments

Thirteen years ago, at the prompting of Karen Lowe, a local newspaper reporter, I began a labor of love on my home computer, capturing stories of my unlikely friendship with HK, and I want to acknowledge the tremendous support I have received in making the publication of our story a reality.

This project became a passion for my friend Andy Hardin, who spent countless hours adding the perfect touches to the manuscript. Without his support, dedication, and belief that we had an inspiring story to share, this project might never have happened.

Being a novice in the publishing world, I had no idea what to expect. I believe it was God's divine guidance that led us to our literary agent, Frank Breeden at Premiere Authors. He willingly read an unknown author's manuscript, confidently provided expert advice in shaping the story, and presented it to the gifted, creative, and dedicated professionals at W Publishing Group. My deepest thanks to the visionary W team, especially Debbie Wickwire, Paula Major, Lori Jones, Lori Cloud, and my coach, Tom Williams.

I'll always be grateful to Pearl, HK, and Brenda for their patience, trust, and encouragement that allowed me to share our story with the world.

—∞—

About the Authors

J IM BRADFORD began a successful sales career with the Xerox Corporation in 1968. He entered the apparel industry in 1983 as the division president of sales for a traditional men's clothing manu- facturer. In 1985, at the invitation of the British Trade Council, he had the honor of presenting a new line of English tailored clothing to HRH Prince Charles and Princess Diana, as part of their royal visit to Washington, DC. Jim has received Rotary's Four Avenues of Service award and served two terms on Nashville's Mayor's Advisory Committee for People with Disabilities. He retired in early 2016 from UniFirst Corporation.

Jim lives in Brentwood, Tennessee, with his wife, Brenda. They have two grown daughters and two grandchildren.

ANDY HARDIN has known Jim Bradford for more than twenty-five years and was part of Jim's Saturday-morning tennis group when Jim first met HK. Jim introduced Andy to HK early in their friendship, and Andy closely followed their adventures throughout the years. After reading Jim's treasured tales of HK's many anecdotes, Andy offered his help to further develop the story. Andy is a retired attorney living in Nashville with his wife, Connie. Their East Tennessee family includes a son, daughter, and six perfectly adorable grandchildren.